Tempus ORAL HISTORY *Series*

Maine Road
voices

Tempus ORAL HISTORY *Series*

Maine Road
voices

Compiled by
Andrew Waldon

First published 2002

Tempus Publishing Limited
The Mill, Brimscombe Port,
Stroud, Gloucestershire, GL5 2QG

ISBN 0 7524 2413 0

Typesetting and origination by
Tempus Publishing Limited
Printed in Great Britain by
Midway Colour Print, Wiltshire

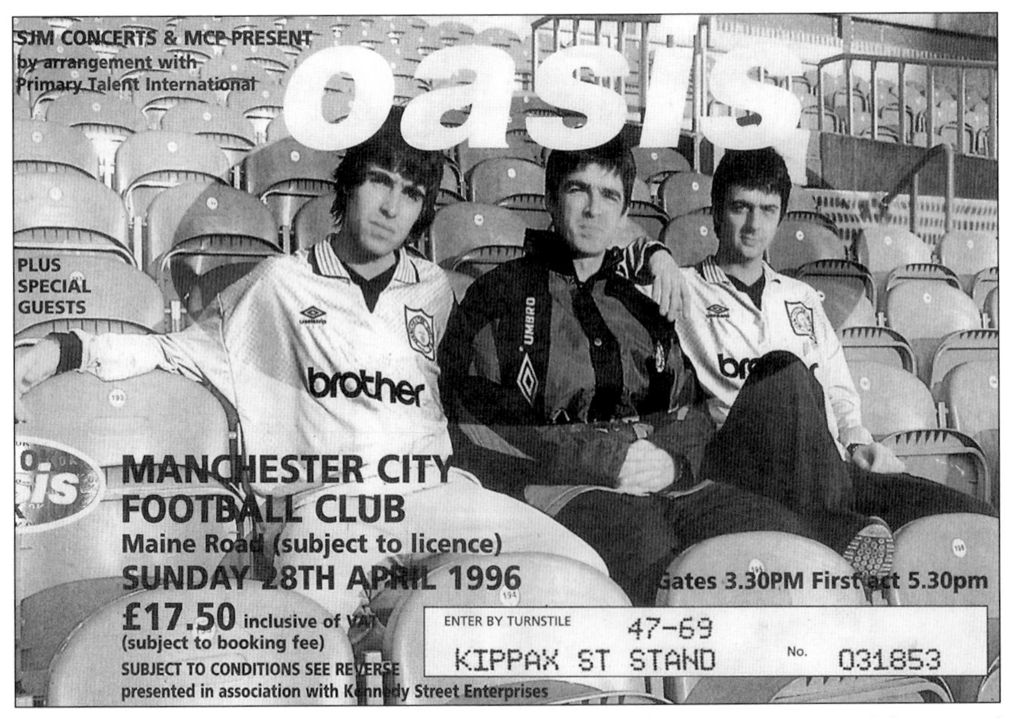

Oasis ticket. Regarded by many as the voice of Maine Road in the 1990s, Oasis spread the name of Manchester City worldwide.

Contents

Acknowledgements

Without the generous help of so many people, this collection of stories and photographs would not have been possible. In particular I would like to thank all the supporters who shared their memories with me and who loaned their treasured photographs and other mementoes for inclusion in this book.

Thanks to Mike Ash, Steve Boyd, Noel Bayley and the boys from *Bert Trautmann's Helmet*, Josh and Worthy (for the use of their photographs), Phil Banerjee, Chris Boyd, Mike Byrne, Jackie Coyle, Julie Clark, Adam Dowell, Carol Darvill, Ken Corfield, Geoff Donkin, Phill Gatenby, Steve Green, John Geary, Mike Holden, Brian Hince, Brad Hamlin, Neil Hughes, Gary James, Craig James, Gary King, Ted Knott, Mike Kelly, Phil Lines, Seamus McAndrew, Joyce Maddocks, Paul Mitchell, Steve Massey, Tony Morgans, Frank Newton, Phil Noble, Peter O'Brien, Wilson Pratt, Brian Prendergast, Ian Penney, Richard Purcell, Mark Redgrave, Phil Rowe, Matthew Roberts, Tom Ritchie, Marc Stein,Gary Stevens, Tim Salt, Daniel Thomas, Andrew Thomas, Peter Talbot, Dave Wallace, Jennifer Wallace, Nick Walker, Tom Welch, Eric Walsh, Bob Young, Frank Williams. Finally, a big thank you to Bernadette Cummings for doing the proofreading (again).

Whilst every attempt has been made to acknowledge the original source of copyright for all pictures in this publication, if anyone has any questions relating to this matter, please contact Tempus Publishing.

Introduction

There are many thousands of loyal supporters of Manchester City Football Club, who come from many different walks of life, and there must be an equal number of stories told by those supporters. This book is about those ordinary fans, and it is their accounts of those memorable moments that feature in the following pages. They cover the highs and the lows, the routine and the idiosyncratic; there are stories of passion, tragedy and humour.

There are many personal anecdotes from fans that tell how Manchester City has played a part in their lives. The theme of this oral history is the passion and loyalty that City fans have for their team.

All City fans will enjoy sharing the experiences recorded here, and in so doing will recall many fond memories of their own.

Andrew Waldon
February 2002

CHAPTER 1

Around Maine Road

A recent aerial view of Maine Road. The new £11 million Kippax Stand towers above everything else.

Views on Maine Road. Is there one point in the ground that you always prefer to watch matches from, where is it and why?

The first ever game I saw was from the Platt Lane. I can't remember who it was against but we were on the back row, sat on wooden benches, and just as the game started, hundreds of people came rushing up the stairs from the back. What stood out was most of them had scarves tied round their wrists or their necks. I can't remember whether they were City fans, or whether this was my first encounter of the famous 1970s football hooligans. I was hooked on City, and as soon as I could afford to, I bought a season ticket for the Kippax. We always stood three-quarters of the way back, always in line with the halfway mark. It was just enough room away to avoid any missiles coming from the segregated area that housed supporters of the opposition, and it always allowed us to be one of the first away on the final whistle, down the steps at the rear exit. Then when the

The end of an era, as demolition begins on the old Platt Lane Stand.

Kippax had to be pulled down, I took up a seat in the North Stand, where the away fans are currently seated. Then I went to the upper tier of the new Kippax. My son then expressed an interest in watching City (not that he had already been brainwashed from the day he was born). So I got two season tickets for the price of one in the Junior Blues stand in the corner of the North Stand, by that open bit with the police control box above it. When the family stand was created in the Platt Lane/Maine Stand corner, we moved there and are still there. But I will always remember the old Kippax.

Andrew Thomas

My memory as a kid was going in the Platt Lane. That's where every kid started off when I was younger. It used to have a singing section at the top of the stand. I was thirteen and wanted to be one of the gang. They all sang up there, but I never made it. I always watch my football from the Kippax now. I once went in the North Stand for one year during the redevelopment of the Kippax. Cracking view, great atmosphere, but just not the same. Sat on the top tier of the Kippax, but it was one of the worst views on the back row, I hated it.

Tom Ritchie

A characteristic part of the Maine Road scene has always been the Platt Lane, with its metal pillars and multi-coloured seats bolted to the original terrace steps. Spectators at the front of the stand often had to stand up to see, and this used to spark off something akin to a Mexican wave; up they'd stand, every time City attacked towards that end of the ground. I always remember climbing up the staircase at the back of the stand and catching my first glimpse of the pitch on match days. In the 1980s, City fans and visiting supporters used to mingle quite peacefully with no segregation necessary. Sadly, towards the end of the '80s, the Platt Lane became a target for a contingent of City troublemakers. Groups of youths, not remotely interested in football, used to wander around the stand during the match looking for trouble, and outbreaks of fighting became an increasingly frequent occurrence. Inevitably, this eventually led to the stand being allocated to away fans only. Many City fans, who had spent years watching the Blues from the Platt Lane were understandably annoyed, especially when they saw pathetically small numbers of visiting supporters often sparsely dotted around, particularly in one cup game against Wimbledon when they had three fans. The Platt Lane was often full to capacity, but how everybody found their seats, I will never know. Block numbers hung from the metal framework of the roof and there was an odd and even numbering sequence, which was very confusing. It was, in my opinion, an important piece of City's history, and I was sad to see it go and be replaced by a more modern, comfortable and expensive 'Umbro' stand. I always used to stand in the corner between the Kippax and the North Stand, even when it was chucking it down with rain. A lot of people referred to it as 'Windy Corner', but we called it 'The Piece of Cake' because of its odd shape.

Gary Stevens

I always could be found in Windy Corner, right at the back of the terracing, leaning

The rear of the new Platt Lane Stand. This stand was formerly known as the Umbro Stand, named after the sportswear manufacturers and one-time provider of City's playing strip.

against the wall. Now I watch my football from the Kippax lower tier.

Peter O'Brien

I am in with the cocoon crowd in Block B of the Maine Stand. There are no kids and it is a very civil crowd, and they do very good Bovril.

Seamus McAndrew

I used to go in the Kippax until the mid-1970s, but it seemed to lose its atmosphere after a bit, and I just liked going in the Maine Stand and have sat more or less in the same place since about 1974, so I am quite used to it in there.

Steve Boyd

It's hard not to get sentimental when talking about the Platt Lane; after all, for many Blues, this is where it all began. In my opinion, the great years of the stand were 1970 to 1978. Many of you will disagree, I'm sure. I honestly don't know what my first City match was. My parents (obsessively Blue) tell me I was about two when they first took me, so it must have been about 1969. All I know is that my earliest memories of City revolve in some way around the Platt Lane stand. For some reason, almost every one of those memories seems to be of a night match, or was it that Platt Lane seemed so dark? I don't know. We used to park miles away, certainly a lot further away than I do today, and yet the atmosphere was electric from the moment we got out of the car. We'd walk down all those passages – you know the ones, they are numbered passage number one, two, seven etc. They seemed to last forever. I remember coming through the tunnel in the

The entrance to Maine Stand – the heart of the club – which is used by so many corporate and VIP guests.

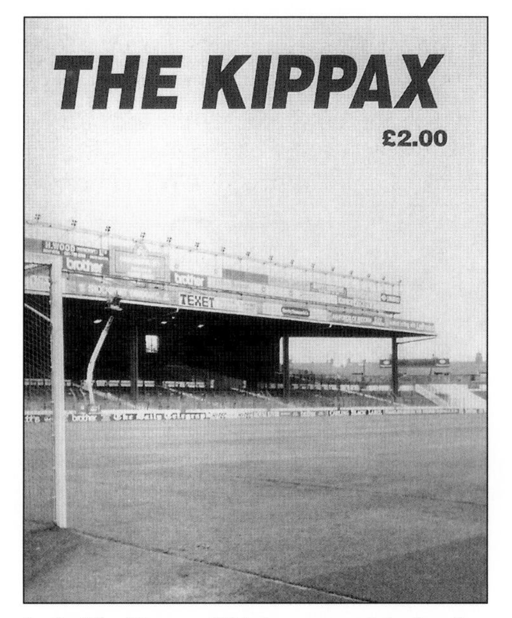

Left: *The Kippax. This is a copy of the brochure produced by the* Electric Blue *fanzine to commemorate the end of the Kippax, due to the implementation of the recommendations of the Taylor Report.* Right: *Standing Ovation brochure. 'A Tribute to the Kippax' was produced by the editorial team of* This Charming Fan, *one of several City fanzines.*

corner with my father and immediately shouting 'CITY!' as if to say 'I'm here, where are you Bell, Lee, Summerbee?' The ground seemed enormous in those days. My father used to take me and my older brother up what seemed like miles of steps to reach our seats. Once seated, my dad would always try to make sure I didn't have a giant in front of me – it was difficult enough seeing from that stand as it was. We would always be kitted out with all the essentials – flask and sandwiches. More often than not, my brother would be responsible for the flask. On at least four occasions that I remember, the flask became a victim of the 'Platt Lane wave' – the strange phenomenon whereby the crowd had to jump up to see the goalmouth action. I first found out what 'season ticket' meant in the Platt Lane. Many of the seats in those days had it written on them. I asked my dad and he explained it all. I was amazed that anyone could afford all that money in one go. My dad always seemed to know someone who sat near. It never seemed to happen in the same way in any of the other stands. In the old days, you often found yourself near an away fan. That was great, unless you were losing. I missed the UEFA Cup game against Widzew Lodz in 1977, but my brother and dad tell me that the Widzew fans caused much amusement by singing and shouting, despite being a goal down. The City fans laughed at them until, in typical style, City allowed them back in the game with a final score of 2-2. Other memories include sneaking in with a bag of chips, because I was told they would throw you out if you did not buy City's pies. I remember Joe Mercer's return as manager of Coventry – what a reception. Then on Boxing Day 1977, there was an

Former stars salute City's last stand . . .

Kippaxed!

by John Scheerhout

THOUSANDS of Manchester City fans bade farewell to their beloved Kippax stand this week.

They sang Blue Moon and gave the old stand a rousing send off in a carnival atmosphere at Maine Road.

A steel band began almost an hour of entertainment by playing some favourite Blues tunes, and thousands of balloons were released in to the sky.

Former stars were paraded on the turf while City's current stars kicked footballs into the crowd.

The fans ensured it was not so much a wake as a party — even though many mourned the passing of the Kippax, which has stood in that corner of Moss Side since 1923.

The Kippax will make way for £30m re-development to comply with the requirements of the Taylor Report. It requires that all the country's top clubs must be all-seater in time for next season after the Hillsborough tragedy.

City drew with Chelsea — but that was secondary. The day really belonged to the Blues' fans and their last stand.

Famous player from City's past — like current chairman Franny Lee, Mike Summerbee and Alex Williams — joined the party for the grand send-off.

Vince Miller led the singing as he does on Cup Final day at Wembley.

Now many of the faithful Kippax fans will have to adjust to the new regime after spending so many years standing to watch and cheer their team.

Kippaxed! A newspaper article about the end of the Kippax.

even greater ovation for Colin Bell coming on the pitch after a couple of years out of the game. Bell was the substitute, and every time he warmed up the crowd got excited. Towards the end of the 1970s, the Platt Lane died for me. I became increasingly disenchanted with the view, and found out by accident one day that whenever I was unable to go to the game, my dad used to take my brother in the more expensive North Stand. I wanted to go there! The Platt Lane is dead now, but I will always remember it as the stand of Bell, Marsh, Mercer and Allison.

Gary James

There has only been one place for me to watch the Blues – the Kippax terrace. In the middle, just to the left of the halfway line (as you look at the pitch.) Maine Road – as with a lot of stadiums with the advent of all-seaters – was never the same after the Kippax terrace was pulled down.

Phill Gatenby

Maine Road, I love it – despite the disastrous ground development. Sometimes, like the rest of you I'm sure, I take a detour just to drive past it and catch a glimpse on my way to work. As a spectator, I've been just about everywhere (except the two Gene Kellys) in the ground, and I find it difficult to understand those fans who complain about their seats being in the wrong area, as I enjoy seeing a game from every possible angle. I started off on the scoreboard end – the only place to be in the 1950s – but saw the odd game from the Kippax, or popular side, as it was then known. I've both sat and stood in the old Platt Lane, the North Stand and Kippax. I've sat in the Umbro, apple pie corner and the Main Stand, where I've also done the executive bit, and I've even sat in the directors' box once, when I was 'Fan on the Board'. I've done the executive box thing in the Platt Lane/Umbro and the Kippax, plus the top tier on one occasion, when I told our Alex (then aged eleven) that we would see the patterns of the game unfold. 'What patterns, Dad?' he said, as we lost 1-0 to lowly Huddersfield. I also stood on Windy Corner for the last day of the Kippax. Currently, I have a fabulous seat at the back of the lower tier of the Kippax. Nothing compares though, with standing on the old Kippax, for the atmosphere, wit, wisdom, singing and chanting. I miss it, as we all do, and also selling fanzines in the tunnels.

Dave Wallace

I started in the Platt Lane as a ten-year-old with my Dad, then went into the old scoreboard end, then changed to the North Stand with standing, and, eventually, when seating was introduced, the corner of the Kippax and North Stand, out in the open. I spent many happy and great years in that corner. It was there I stood for the Kippax's last stand, and spent a long time reliving great memories for the last time, then I went back to the Platt Lane before being temporarily in the North Stand, while waiting for my new seat in the Kippax upper tier, where I now reside. They will, when that fateful day arrives, have to carry me out screaming and kicking, as I for one still don't know why we have to move to Eastlands. I know, as I once saw plans for it, that they can re-build Maine Road to seat 50,000. So many memories of good and bad times will be lost when we move!

Mike Ash

My favourite view of the ground is from the roof of the Kippax, which I enjoyed when abseiling from the floodlights with City mascot 'Moonchester' for the Marie Curie Cancer Charity, a couple of years ago!

Ian Cheeseman

A view from the car park of the new Kippax.

Two pictures showing the development of City's new stadium in Eastlands, Manchester, which will be known as The City of Manchester Stadium.

CHAPTER 2

Cup Trial

Hovercraft ticket – the beginning of a journey.

Let's pause for a minute and think about the European Cup-winners' Cup, FA Cup, League Cup, Auto Windscreen Trophy, UEFA Cup and so on, and recall some of the most significant matches.

The Road To Valencia

It was summer 1972. I had been working for ICI for two years, making blue pigments for a living so that we could colour everything the right way, still broke and no holiday to look forward too. And then the news all City fans needed: the UEFA cup draw! Valencia in September. I saw all my mates on the Kippax, as City typically lost the first home match of the season 0-1 to Everton, and asked them who fancied going to Spain. These veterans of Holland, West Germany, Belgium, and still rich enough to go to Vienna while I was too broke to go, all had other things to do! But I was twenty and wanted adventure and a passport. The photo booth was invaded and I spent the next ten years being thoroughly embarrassed at Passport Controls around Europe. Anyway, I had decided to watch City in Valencia (second leg) and make it a week's holiday hitch-hiking at great expense – I reckoned £30 should get me there and back. I drew all I had out of the bank and pleaded with them to change some into pesetas, not an easy thing to do before package tours took off.

John Geary's passport photo....or is this Count Dracula?

OK, maybe I was sacrificing my HNC studies at John Dalton, but we are only young once. Of course, by the time of the first leg at Maine Road, City were slumped at the foot of the table. Valencia were not famous then either, but had more about them than we did, and a 2-2 draw was the best we could do. I didn't go to Spain worrying that a victory could leave me exposed to danger though; it seemed too unlikely the way Valencia had played. I found a small Union Jack and got my Mum to sew it on the rucksack to help me get lifts, and set off for Altrincham. Amongst the stuff I packed was a load of strong polythene from work (we had some perks) to make a bivouac tent when stuck in the middle of nowhere, and, expecting that idea to fail, my International YHA membership, for those comforts I would miss. And £30 – would that be enough? It had to be in the days before credit cards and exchange rates always made you feel a loser, but nevertheless, some was in francs and a little in pesetas. Why Altrincham? It was my traditional route out of town on a Friday night when City were in London, or visiting my Man City mates who were clever enough to have gone to Oxford. I would get the last train from Mauldeth Road, changing at Oxford Road to get the electric to Alti, or did they go straight through by then? Then a short walk to the edge of town and a wait for the traffic flowing down the Chester Road to pick me up and drop me at Tabley for a lorry down the M6. (I once cycled to Chester and back to watch City with my friend Pete in a pre-season friendly, but that's another story and not a recommendation). So, I kept to the tried and trusted method. and by four o'clock in the morning, I was on the M1 in the Newport Pagnall services and hit London with the Saturday morning shoppers. Hitching across London was always a waste of time, so the Tube was used and the Elephant & Castle was the target to go on to Kent. Now in new territory for me, I enjoyed the last days of an English summer, it being a lot warmer down South. Eventually, the miserable Southerners got round to giving me a lift the last few miles to Dover (amazing how your impressions of people are altered by the side of a dual carriageway) and I found another new adventure to go on – the Seaspeed Hovercraft. Looking round for all the other City fans I thought were bound to be gathering here for the epic journey to the land of oranges and paella, I was quietly disappointed, mainly because there were none and hence no one to talk to. Perhaps they were all watching City, I thought, as it was about six-ish and we did have a game against somebody, but I can't remember who.

I took my seat on the strange contraption, obviously a British invention akin to 'Chitty, Chitty, Bang, Bang', and watched Blighty slip away. (It wasn't long after the war and I felt as though I was single-handedly taking on Europe in my first-ever journey from England!) Well, I would have done, but for the spray the damn things generate. Thank God that cats and tunnels have replaced them! A shock awaited me on the other side, in Calais. Everybody was foreign and I hadn't a clue where to go. My attempts at passing French 'O' Level should have involved more effort, as three fails doesn't help much when it has suddenly gone dark, there are no street lights and you can hear strange noises similar to those on Santana's Caravanserai LP (crickets). I wandered, fortunately, straight into Calais and out the other side, apparently going South. A group of Froggies, seeing me try to thumb a lift, decided to harangue me, but my lack of French worked to my advantage, and I couldn't insult them enough to provoke a fight, so they went for reinforcements. Then a lift! But where to? A field in Northern France. Dropped off in the middle of nowhere, I jumped over a gate and settled down for the night. Forget about cows and snakes and things. Wrapped up in my best polythene and in the sleeping bag cosily snoring after a few minutes, but then it was cold, and later *bloody* cold and damp. Condensation everywhere, and what was that smell, and bloody great thing looming in the dark? Yes, it's a cow. Great. Now what, turn over and wait for the sun, at least there's no frost. Then up, and with no breakfast, start thumbing. My first impressions of Northern France were that it consists of ninety per cent doctors driving souped-up Renault 12s or dotty 2 CVs. However, I soon found out the whole of France seemed like this to hitchhikers. I meandered my way past patisseries and conficières (no decent chippies, note) through Abbeville, Beauvais and luckily around Paris quickly on the Perepherique and out on the N20 to Etampes, then reaching Orleans by nightfall. But, no point in stopping, a long way to go and on into the night, still busy roads on a Sunday, doing well to reach Limoges at midnight, and only the railway station open. Mixed in with the conscript soldiers travelling who knows where, I enjoyed my first taste of real French coffee in ridiculous small cups at massive prices – not too much of that

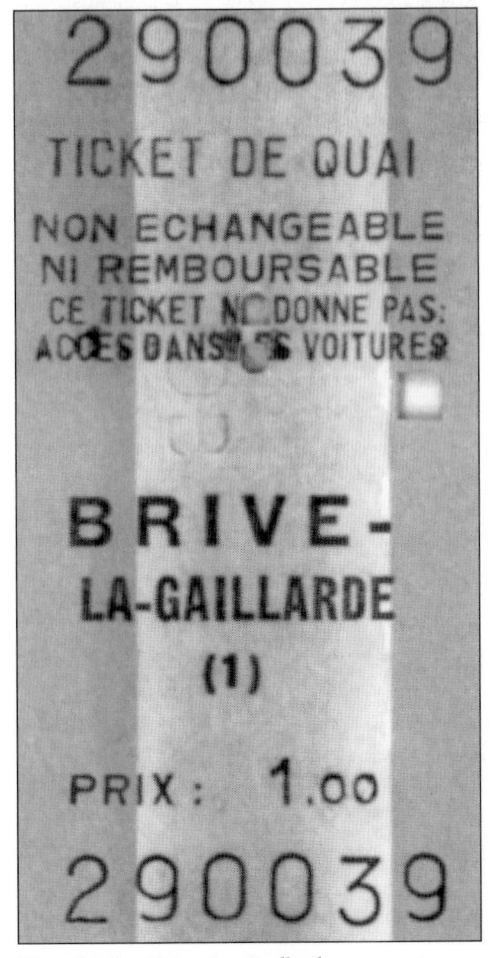

Travel ticket Brive-La Gaillarde

Travel ticket Lerida-Tarragona

then. No real sleep, too many guns about and by 7 a.m. back on the N20 to Brive, now a famous Rugby Union town. Big, strong blokes who have a taste for ears and singing bawdy songs. More doctors. Out of the town and it's getting warm again. And a BMW draws up, nice bloke, very friendly. Suddenly, we are in a lay-by and he's too friendly, his hand stroking my leg, I grab my rucksack, do my best to punch him and run for it, all in a blur. But it's a long way from any where, and I don't know how determined he is to follow me. I don't see him following though, maybe he turned back? Soon a lorry driver stops. Am I glad to get out of here – I dare not dwell on what might have happened. Or how a woman would feel in those circumstances. Forty miles later, I worry a lot less, but ignore all the BMWs in future, too much room in the front. I find myself by a hot dusty road near Montauban. First time out of England, it feels like I am in the African desert. Luckily, Coca-Cola has got here, and every garage has a chilled machine, so I could get a taste for it, if I had the francs. Starting to worry now that I won't get there in time. It isn't too difficult to get the lifts, but a lot aren't big distances and I have to get through Toulouse without losing a day. My trusty Michelin map rarely tells me where I am, the detail of such a big country isn't on it. Luckily, Toulouse is a big, busy city and I'm soon on the other side heading on this magical journey for the Pyrenees! Darkness is falling quicker this far south, and as I reach the foothills, all goes black, and I find myself still on the N20 in a small town called Foix. Hungry, I head for a small bar, (café-bar to us now). The strange people inside could be from Transylvania. Everyone else knows each other and they keep pointing at me as if I am Count Dracula, or at least the blond-haired virgin being readied for the vampire. Even the village has all the landmarks: little bridge, nearby forest, little electricity, wind (in me). I walk a little way from the centre out onto the main road, but there's little traffic. A bus shelter looms out of the gloom and it isn't too cold and, paradise, it has a bench seat large enough to lie on. I tidy up my belongings and settle for a draughty night, thinking to set my alarm for an early start. 7 a.m. and the traffic wakes me up. Lorries grinding up the hill, people waiting for a bus, strange looks again. I am quite an expert on UK lorries, after numerous motorway journeys to watch City. Scania are favourites for comfort, Renault are big, and Fiat and DAF come with some comfort too. But not AEC or Seddon! This was a Fiat stopping, and he's going to Lerida, that's all the way over the top and well into Spain. We exchange signs about lunch, football, and that's it, no conversation expected or needed, sit back and enjoy the journey. This is what hitching should be like. We climb ever upwards, as the u-bends are negotiated; the heat in the cab oscillates from very warm in the sun to very chilly in the shade. It looks like the Lake District near the top, green and craggy.

But then at the border we stop for a bite to eat, and I'm offered what looks like raw ham. Fine time to pick up a bug, so I decline and eat a chocolate biscuit, and wish crisps had been exported here. (This could be a new venture for me when I set up a crisp-exporting business on my return.) Dropping down off the high mountains, the colourful flowers and lush valleys are a complete surprise, must revisit them. But back on the road, the story changes, and he has to use every inch of the barrier-less roads to scare me to death before dropping me off in Dead Man's Gulch, or so it seems. Too many westerns were shot in Spain, and I've seen most of them. Transit vans and flies are the memories of the last hundred miles to Lerida, and then orange lorries and siesta to while away the evening, still short of time with the match next day. McDonald's hadn't reached anywhere in 1972, never mind Spain, so eating was a problem on the road. Coffee and buns in cafes were often the only items on my menu. It was the same in Lerida, and I was hungry as I settled down outside the cop-shop in the town centre, another nice area of flower-strewn parkland with big benches. Before sleeping, I had located the railway station and noted the train times, as I couldn't afford to get stranded in the middle of nowhere on the day of the match. So when I awoke early, of course, on the day of the game, I soon found myself in a two-car diesel on my way to Tarragona. Sounds easy doesn't it, but I missed out the section on buying a ticket, i.e. my first real Spanish conversation. And for about twenty pence I got to ride with cats, dogs and donkeys for about fifty miles to the coast, and soon friendly Spaniards continually pointed at my long blond hair and giggled. The Tarragonese were just the same and I crossed the bridge over the dried-up river bed to the main road to Valencia, now just straight down the coast road. Not far

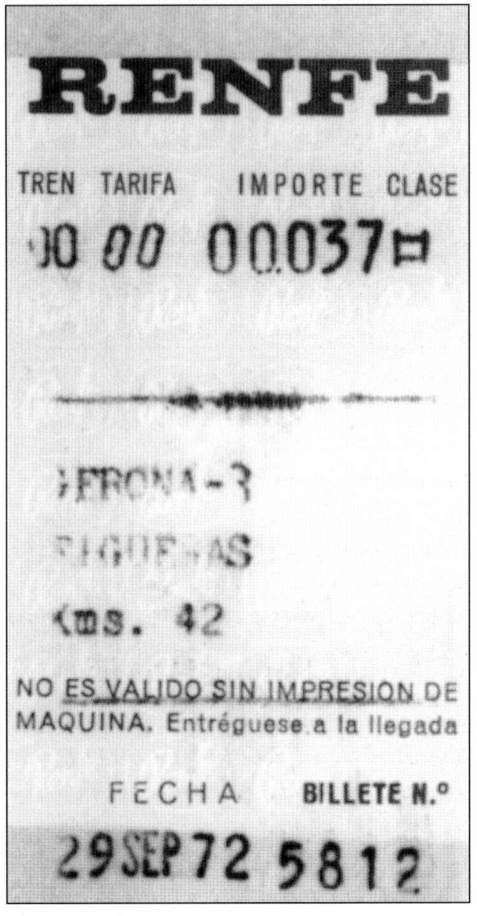
RENFE

TREN TARIFA IMPORTE CLASE

00 00.037

Kms. 42

NO ES VALIDO SIN IMPRESION DE MAQUINA. Entréguese a la llegada

FECHA BILLETE N.º

29SEP72 5812

Travel ticket Gerona-Figueras – a journey costing twenty pence.

IT'S SO TOUGH ON BATTLING BLUES

Headline from Manchester Evening News *on the game against Valencia.*

now, with a golden beach and blue sea like I'd never seen before glimpsed from the road, and a couple of Renault 12s later, I was there, wandering around the beautiful city finding Blues speckled here and there. Pavement cafes and bars abound, though I was worried at first that most seemed shut. Had our reputation preceded us? What reputation? We hadn't been in Europe that much. No, simply siesta time and I was ignorant of it. I easily found the ground; I have a nose for them, and spotted an entrance into the stadium that was open! Security was not the same there as now. A polite groundsman escorted me off the premises as far as the ticket office, and I bought a ticket for the front row behind the North goal (£2.20). Back outside, the Spanish were learning to drive (at last, I thought) and at least it utilized the car park during the day. I wandered back into town, secure in the knowledge that I was at least going to get in the ground. Now I needed a bed for the night. In a side street, the familiar songs were wafting towards me ('Fly over Stretford' etc.) and I found loads of Blues drinking the afternoon away, everyone hailing me as a hero after my intrepid journey overland. They had mostly flown in, with a few coach travellers. One of the Moston branch (Gardener's Arms) of the supporters' club (Ian Thompson?) offered me a floor for the night, and after an hour or two of merriment, I found myself in a small hotel waiting for the coaches to take us to the ground. This was style after the hitching, and everyone was looking after my needs – we are such a friendly bunch. Then it was 7 p.m. and I was smuggled onto the coach after a lot of counting numbers in Spanish. At the ground I was still a little drunk, but not as bad as the rest, and managed to arrange to meet them at the coach to keep together. I received many admiring glances from men and women as I took my seat, and I realised just how odd I must look to the average Spaniard. At least there was no pretending not to be English, and they didn't seem too hostile. An old bloke was sitting next to me, and he soon gave up trying to talk to me, but he insisted I shared his butties, which helped to break the ice with all the Spaniards surrounding me. Where were all the Blues then? City had been held to a 2-2 draw at home, so not a lot was expected of us away. And that was what we got, with Valencia strolling into a 2-0 lead. An abiding memory of the game, as I sobered up a little, was the incredible number of bottles City fans were able to throw into the home crowd, way over to my left. Where did they find them all? My friends (now) sitting with me didn't seem too appalled by our behaviour, but it annoyed me that we would attract a different kind of support to games that some fans attended for all the wrong reasons, repeated thirty years later, when many part-time City fans turned up too drunk to watch and support the team properly against Gillingham at Wembley. Just before the ninety minutes were up, Rodney got a tap in right in front of me and I nodded and winked at him, and said 'see you in the bar later'! Soon the police were everywhere, shepherding us onto buses, but as I was going to stay the night, I managed to meet my new mates and escape from the buses to head for the bars. Steel and chrome came early to Spanish nightlife, though we soon found the seedier side. Small, old women seemed to take a particular fancy to my long blond hair, but I turned down all their offers, I didn't have money for that. 'Tommy' Doyle and Rodney Marsh (without socks of course) joined us for a post-match post mortem and many a drink was had, but I still found myself on the hotel room floor early next morning. I bade farewell to my Blue mates and headed for the coast road; I had work to get back for on Monday. I was still attracting strange men from building sites on the coast road back north, and the blond hair made it difficult to get lifts all day in Spain, as they know you are foreign! Had a great one through Barcelona at nightfall, with so much heavy traffic and lots of Spanish girls gesticulating at me. I ended up near the youth hostel in Gerona and a quiet night in was had. Another early start, but no lifts and I was struggling now, so I started cheating and got the train to Figueras (twenty pence) at the border and reached Perpignan by nightfall. (I had opted for an alternative route back, as the Pyrenean way I came seemed too remote for good hitching going north.) More traffic used the coast road and I suddenly got lucky. A young Belgian couple picked me up and we travelled through the night all the way up the Rhone valley, past Montpelier, Avignon, Lyon and up through Troyes and finally reaching the famous prison town of St Quentin in the early afternoon. That was the best lift I ever had, and after this trip I virtually retired from the boredom of hitchhiking. Saturday evening, beginning to get really hungry and fed up of the uncertainty of hitching, so I took a slow train to Amiens, and seemed to spend most of the night there. Then the train to Boulogne was the answer. I crossed the

This is a real collector's item – a ticket from the game played against Valencia at the Estadio Luis Casanova.

channel in discomfort on the hovercraft again at 11.30 a.m. Sunday morning, with the total hovercraft cost being £6.60. Soon I was on the train to London, and then heading north on the coach from Victoria.

For anoraks like me:

Hitchhiked – 2,202 miles
Walked – 38 miles
Train – 393 miles
Coach – 198 miles
Bus – 13 miles
Hovercraft – 53 miles

TOTAL – 2,897 miles

John Geary

It's A Kind Of Magic

I have had some great times at Old Trafford, many good high scores in our favour. The night Mike Summerbee hit an indirect free-kick at Alex Stepney, who in turn pushed it into the roof of his net, and we had won the League Cup semi-final (4-3 on aggregate) – the scenes were incredible, inside and out. Who could ever forget Denis Law's back-heel to relegate his old team, and the wry smile he gave which told us he had not regretted what he had done? Or the two pitch invasions that followed, eventually leading to the game being unable to continue – how gentlemanly our friends from Salford were that day. But the best ever was a night in either late March or April. We were 1-0 down to a goal by Best after only about five minutes. The Reds were going wild, I was fourteen, never been to a derby at Old Trafford before. We were in the United Road paddock, there was this big guy stood behind me nudging and shouting in my face about how great they were, and we had no right to be challenging for their title! Well, what an idiot! The game rolled on, big George Heslop equalized for us then, I think, if I have it the right way round. 'God' or Colin Bell put us in front, and I think he was through again when he was brought down in the area, I actually think he went off injured, but I'm not sure on this. Anyway, Franny (Lee) stepped up to take it and five seconds later we were in ecstasy – game, set and title! I was pushing my scarf in this big fella's face, and the adult I had gone with was pulling me off him, he wouldn't hit a kid but he might've hit the adult. The scenes were magical outside – the Reds were too sick to start any trouble and there were too many Blues. Anyhow, they had witnessed the end of their reign at that time; today, unfortunately, it's a different story.

Mike Ash

The most significant game in recent years has got to be the 1999 play-off final, because if we had not won that, I think we might have struggled to get out of that division for another couple of years. In terms of an actual occasion, I enjoyed the FA Cup Final reply of 1981, even though we lost it. It just seemed such a momentous occasion, both games, and we never expected to get there after the way the team had been struggling. I was gutted when Tommy Hutchinson deflected the free-kick past Corrigan in the first game. For some reason, I was not as upset in the second game. It was such a great game of football, with its ups and downs, I just got caught up in everything.

Steve Boyd

Through The Puddles

For many of us, Ninian Park was a new ground to visit, one which could be crossed off the list. We should have known better In the week before the game, almost everyone I spoke to said pretty much the same thing: 'You'll have to watch it down there. They're barmy'. Surely it could not be that bad, could it? Of course, I'd heard about the trouble Cardiff fans were involved in at Fulham and in Greece, and can there be anybody who is not aware of the trouble that flares up whenever Cardiff meet their arch enemies, Swansea City? The van arrived at Worthy's house before eight o'clock, so we could get down to South Wales in good time and have a few pints. Much of what I had heard in the preceding week had been forgotten, as the cans of Boddies and funny cigarettes were passed around the van. At the Severn Bridge, Bibby said we would be better off going into Newport rather than Cardiff itself. He had been there before, but I was not too happy. After all, I had fanzines to sell, war zone or not, and no one else was too bothered where we went for a pint, so Cardiff it was. With that, we drove straight to the ground and parked up, about 100 yards from Ninian Park's Grandstand. It was only about twelve o'clock as we picked our way through the puddles, walked across the car park and round the ground in search of the nearest pub. On past the Ninian Park pub we walked, and about ten minutes later we found another pub. Apart from a dozen or so Cardiff fans, the place was empty. It was also dark and dingy, and the windows had been replaced so many times there was not a single pane of glass that matched another. The beer wasn't worth drinking either, but the atmosphere was convivial enough and before long, City and Cardiff fans alike were mixing and chatting with each other. I left at about quarter to two to make my way to the ground. Completely unhindered on the ten-minute walk, I recognized the familiar scenes that small towns and cities are party to whenever a David and Goliath cup-tie is in the offing. As fathers pinned rosettes onto their bewildered offspring and young lads hastily bought scarves from fly-by-night vendors, unbeknown to me, there was quite a fight in full swing outside the very pub that I had left only minutes earlier. Still, that's the magic of the cup for you. Rounding the corner of Sloper Road and walking behind the away end – Grange End Terrace – I saw one or two familiar faces, but I was struck by a more unfamiliar feeling in the air. I quickly found a spot to stand in, while half-a-dozen stewards, whose job it was to point both City fans and Cardiff's new-found 10,000-plus fans alike to their appropriate turnstiles, stood behind me. The number of Cardiff fans who tried to buy a fanzine from me in the belief they were the official programme was, quite simply, unbelievable. One lad of about twenty walked towards me in his yellow and green United shirt and I said to him 'You're at the wrong ground, aren't you?' and his girlfriend replied: 'Well, Ryan Giggs is from Manchester, isn't he?' While most of the Cardiff fans that came my way were equally as unintelligent, many had come with more sinister objectives on their minds than hoping to catch a glimpse of Ryan Giggs. A worrying trend was evidently unfolding in front of me, but not, it seemed, in front of the police or stewards, who remained oblivious to everything around them. Groups of a dozen or so Cardiff fans would walk amongst the few Blues who had turned up early, clearly trying to provoke the odd one or two into what would have been a hopelessly one-sided brawl. These pathetic charades went

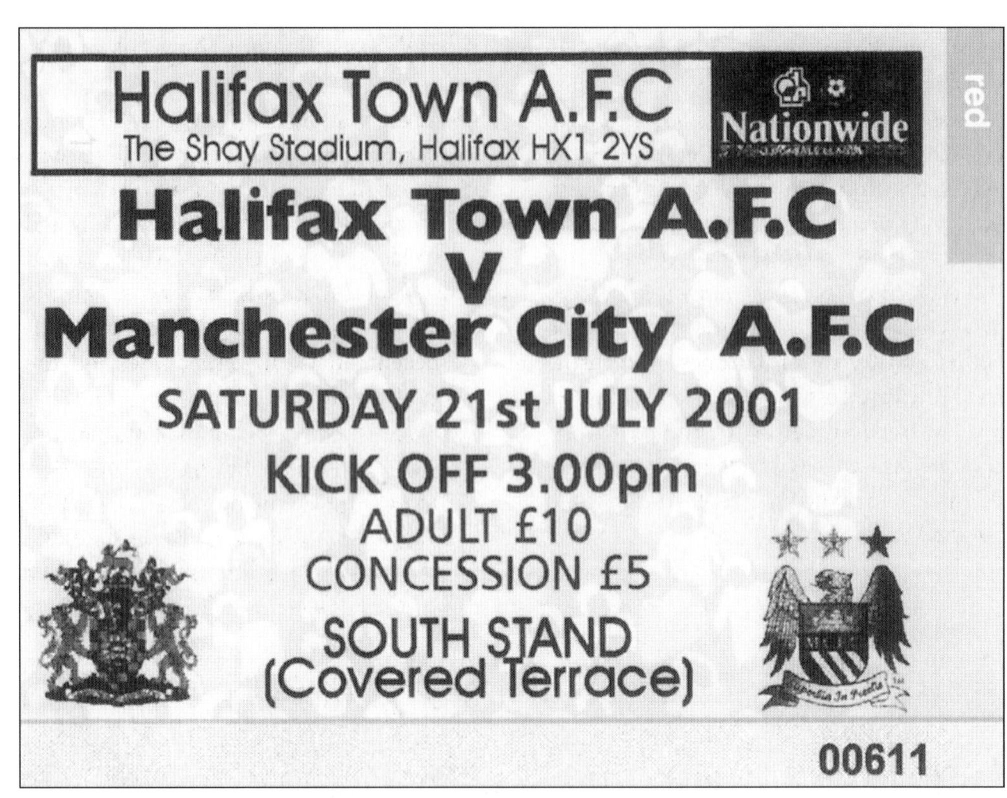

A ticket stub from a pre-season friendly against Halifax.

on for the best part of an hour before the kick-off. Whilst we saw this particular match as a FA Cup tie, I was told that it had been hyped all week by the local media as an international match – England *v.* Wales. The police simply were not clued up, and were content to stand around and smile. Then twenty minutes before the kick-off, about fifty or sixty Cardiff fans had lined up in the middle of the street in readiness to charge towards the City end, and a handful of mounted officers were forced to move to disperse them. It was at this point that I decided to call it a day, I was inside the ground at ten to three, and inside Cardiff and City fans were baying at each other through a wire fence beside the turnstiles. Predictably City tried playing it safe, and with that the outcome was inevitable. Too many players were either uninterested or just not up to the task in hand that particular afternoon. Time and time again over the years, City teams have gone out looking for a draw and come off second-best. This occasion was no exception, and it was the latest sorry addition to an unenviable list that includes trips to Halifax, Brentford, Blackpool, and probably many more. Although many of the lads standing near me at Ninian Park would have gladly settled for a draw, if only to take the Cardiff fans on in the back streets around Maine Road. Why do City never play to win against supposedly inferior opposition? Keith Curle may have been unlucky to have had a goal disallowed, a penalty saved and a last-gasp shot saved, but those incidents apart, nobody other than Tony Coton and Terry Phelan looked remotely interested. Despite repeated requests over the tannoy system not to invade the pitch, Cardiff fans swarmed all over it at the final whistle. Not content with the win or simply to gloat, they came over to the Grange end to goad and provoke. I'd had enough, I did not bother to wait for the gates to open and I certainly was not going to bother and try to sell fanzines. A turnstile had been forced open and some of us climbed over it. I dodged out of the way of Cardiff fans and walked slowly across the car park, through the puddles and back to the van, a hundred yards away.

Noel Bayley

The Worst Day Of My Life

It had been raining all week, and even when we arrived at the ground, it was still bucketing it down, but still we took up our places in the paddock, squashed like sardines and took a look at the pitch. To say it was a mud bath is probably an understatement. The first half was so bad that I cannot remember a single decent attack by either side, and the second half started like that too. Well, that was until about ten minutes from the end, and then Halifax had their one and only shot in the game and – unbelievably – it went in. Pandemonium set in, not just on the pitch but the terraces too. City realised they had a game on their hands, and both Steve Daley

A ticket stub from City's first game back against Halifax at The Shay after the embarrassing FA Cup defeat.

and Bobby Shinton were guilty of missing easy chances. Well, when the final whistle went, the whole place just erupted, as frustrated City fans took their anger out not just on the players, but anything else that moved. Outside the ground, a gang of Blues tried to wreck the team bus. We vowed we would never be back at such a shambles of a ground – well, that was until pre-season a couple of years ago, when all the memories came flooding back.

Tim Salt

I would have to say the two games against Everton in the quarter-final of the FA Cup in 1981. The game at Goodison we knew would be difficult (and I include getting there and back in one piece too!). City were losing 2-1 with not too long to go, when Paul Power raced clear and lobbed the goalie – it seemed to take forever bouncing along, before hitting the back of the empty net. Those Blues behind the goal could see it going in, whilst those of us in the side paddock endured a few more seconds of agony before replacing it with ecstasy! The replay was a walkover, with Bobby MacDonald (two goals) and Dennis Tueart scoring in a spectacular performance. The atmosphere that night was something special, we just knew we could make it to the final after that ... and just hoped we could win it ...

Phill Gatenby

Another Heroic Failure

I doubt if many Blues would plump for the 1981 FA Cup Final as being one of their worst memories, but I certainly would – let me explain. For me, the 1980/81 season was strange if nothing else. In all the time I've been watching City, that was the only season when I only went to a handful of games, although I can't quite remember why that was. Perhaps it was the fact that I had little money and most of my school friends had lost interest – so ensuring that match days were something of a solitary experience – but even so, nothing quite captures the lapsed fan's imagination like a good cup run, does it? Again, I have to pass on that one too, as apart from the thrilling 6-0 victory over Norwich in the fourth round, the magic of the FA Cup failed to lure me again until we got to the final itself. Nobody of my age at the time (fourteen) travelled regularly (if at all) then, and even so, each and every car heading off for the bright lights and subsequent glories that were Goodison and Villa Park were filled to the brim. My semi-final day was spent sitting anxiously in front of the radio until Paul Power clinched a cup final place in extra time. I decided there and then that I was going to the final. After all, my season ticket guaranteed me a Wembley ticket, but transport and money would again be something of a problem. It sounds ridiculous now, but I sent off my £3.50 for a standing ticket along with the voucher and waited for my centenary cup final ticket to arrive, despite being convinced that it would get lost in the post. I'll never forget the relief that the postman brought several days later, but with that relief came a fresh anxiety: where would I keep the ticket safe? what if the house burned down? what if we were burgled? One of the stereo's speakers provided the ticket with the perfect safekeeping place, although what security it would have provided from both fire and theft, I cannot say. You might think I was being unduly paranoid now, but almost every night there was some City fan or other

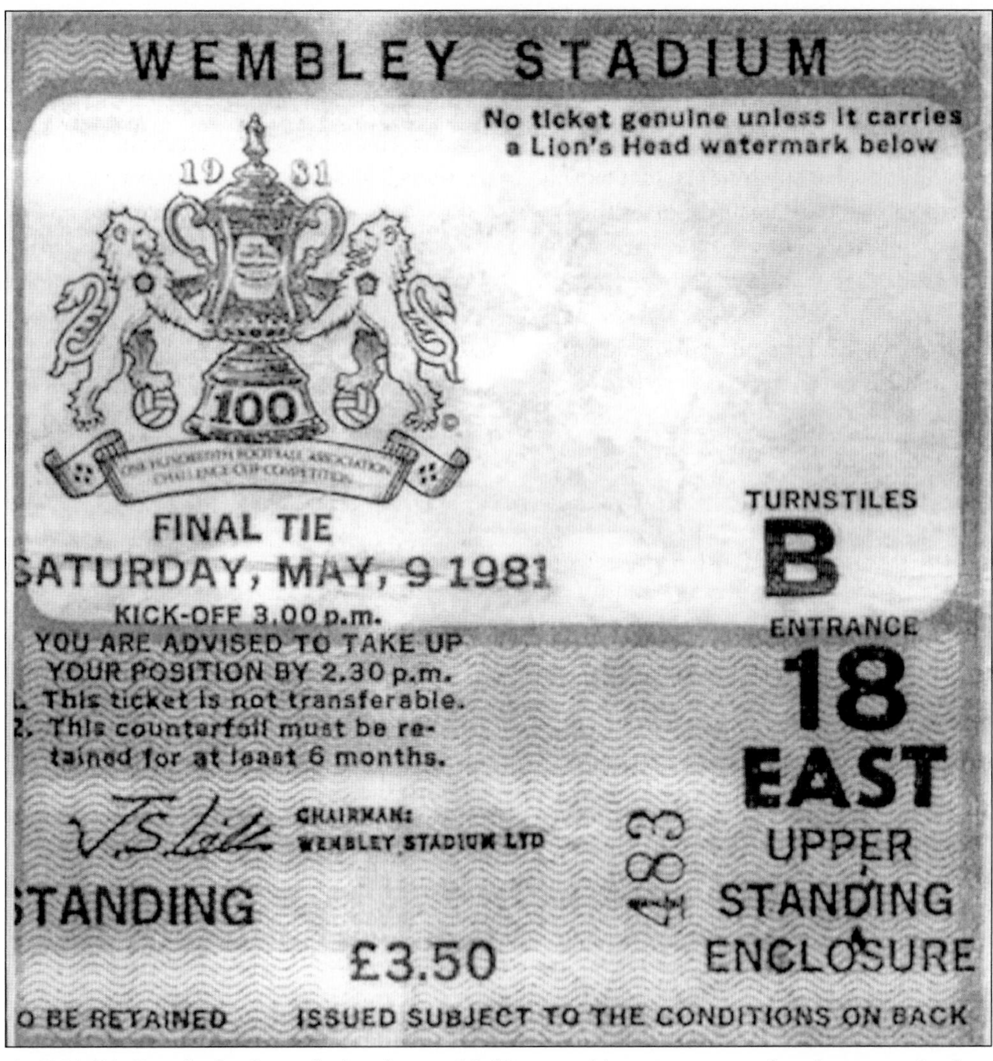

A 1981 FA Cup final ticket, which only cost £3.50 – a real bargain compared to the prices of today.

in the *Evening News* holding up a mush that had previously been a cup final ticket, while one fan's budgie (Asa) soon made short work of his. Having sorted out travel arrangements with a friend of my parents, there was nothing to stop me going, but as the big day got nearer and the hype built up, I just hoped that I would not miss the bus to Stockport station, or worse still, get hit by the bus. I was up early on cup final morning – at about six o'clock, just to make sure and to unscrew the speaker. Still taking no chances, I put the ticket in a plastic bag inside my boot. It was bloody uncomfortable, but worth it all the same, and there it stayed until we got to Wembley. The talk on the train revolved mainly around the twin threat of Steve Archibald and Garth Crooks, although I couldn't see it myself as they'd only scored three apiece in the seven games that had taken Spurs to Wembley. Spurs were favourites, year of the cockerel and all that, and nobody but us believed that we had any chance of winning. The walk from Wembley Central was a long and unfamiliar one and, for some reason, amid all the banter and hurly burly, we went into the local Woolworth's where I bought a book by Stephen Piles: *The Book of Heroic Failures.* Approaching the stadium, City and Spurs fans mingled freely, with no signs of trouble, which was unusual for those days. When we arrived at Wembley, a couple of enterprising City fans threw a rope and grapple up towards a walkway between the twin towers. How successful they were I don't know, and we headed towards the East End to wait for the gates to open. One City fan on the steps next to me had a couple of cans of Boddies that hadn't travelled too well, and whilst opening one of them, he managed to drench me. Eager to make amends, he handed the can over, and not wishing to appear ungrateful, I sampled the far-from-delightful experience of lukewarm Boddies for the first time, as I battled to get the ticket out of my boot, much to the amusement of all and sundry. Once inside Wembley, it wasn't long before the fun and games started with the highlight being a model aircraft display team, one of whom narrowly missed decapitating Tony Book with his plane, when previous captains were wheeled out onto the pitch. I must have been inside Wembley for five hours all told, but it flew by, or, at least, it flew by until the second half of normal time. The feeling that we were winning and so near to picking up the cup was incomparable, despite the fact that I'd accidentally been given a thick lip by someone's flagpole when Hutchison scored his 'first'. The second half seemed to get longer, and soon after we'd applauded the forlorn figure of Ricky Villa round the pitch and down the tunnel (well, how were we to know?) and as the men in white coats high up in the scoreboard started to get restless, Keith Hackett awarded Spurs a free-kick against Gerry Gow. I couldn't bear to look, and didn't. But in the space of seconds, the FA Cup was out of reach, lost as only City could ever lose it. You could argue that things might have been different if Bond had given Tueart a start, if Mackenzie hadn't missed with that glorious opportunity or if we'd have played just forty minutes each way. I often think of that moment when we relinquished our lead and everything that went with it. I don't just mean Europe or the pictures in the paper or any of that, but this was City's golden opportunity – and the last to date – and they blew it. I'm convinced that things would have been different but for those last ten minutes, but who could say otherwise. Unfortunately, we'll never know.

Noel Bayley, editor of Man City fanzine Bert Trautmann's Helmet

The Fog

The most bizarre game I have witnessed in all the thirty years I have been watching City took place in 1978. It was a UEFA Cup tie: away, against AC Milan. As one of a party of four, I flew early on the Wednesday morning for the game, which was due to kick off at eight o'clock that evening. After being overtaken by Concorde, it was bright sunshine that greeted us at Milan airport. We were taken to our hotel, where we changed and then made our way to one of the many roadside bars. It was here that we grasped the language fluently, and in remarkable time: 'Quattro beero, please'. At around four o'clock, one of the locals entered the bar and approached us. 'You boys over for the game?' he asked. 'Yes' we replied in unison. 'Game off' he says. 'Off, what are you talking about?' He went on: 'Fog. Fog come down from mountains, game off'. Quick as a flash, we all rushed to the nearest window. The sun was still shining brightly and we could literally see for miles. 'Oh yes, very funny', we said. The local was still adamant: 'No, no it's off – fog.' About 6.30 p.m. the coach arrived to take us to the ground. Within an hour, the aforementioned fog had made its appearance. We were dropped off about thirty yards from the ground, and we could not see a single brick of the massive San Siro walls. We eventually made our way in, and all we could see were hazy images of the many fires started on the terracing to keep the Milan fans warm. Any hint of green grass was completely out of the question. There were many announcements over a high quality public address system; the only thing was, not one of them was in English. After what seemed an eternity – it was probably ninety minutes or so – we were finally told that there was no chance of play that night. We were then told to go to the ticket office, where we could get replacement tickets for the rearranged fixture tomorrow, kick-off 12 noon. Because our return flight was at two o'clock, this put us in a tricky position. We could either miss the second half or miss our flight. At half-time, the Blues were leading 2-0. We decided the game was ours and it was safe to get the flight back. The coach back to the airport was driven by a Milan supporter who had a

Dave Watson exchanges pennants before the match against Milan in the San Siro Stadium.

City players celebrate by showing off the FA Cup with a lap of honour, after a thrilling final, played on a quagmire of a pitch.

television over his rear view mirror, and spent the entire trip watching the second half. Great, we thought, we wouldn't miss anything. We nearly missed everything when Milan pulled a goal back. The driver leapt from his seat and began jumping around in the aisle. Cries of 'Would you kindly sit down please' (or similar) came from every seat on the coach. Just before we boarded the plane, Milan equalized and the leg finished 2-2. Only City fans could travel all the way to Italy for forty-five minutes of football!

Ian Penney, author of Blue Heaven

The Letter

I wasn't really travelling to see City in the early days of my support (late 1960s), so my most significant cup matches would have to be the FA Cup Final in 1981 and the replay, where me and Maggie ended up in the Spurs end wearing our colours – one woman wanted to nick my blue and white teddy, but gave us both some grub instead! Also the Full Members' Cup Final, which we lost to Chelsea, 5-4 – John and Joyce came that day (we drove down after the 1-1 draw at Old Trafford the day before), they disappeared to the car park at 5-1 down and couldn't believe it when Maggie and I strolled back to say the score was 5-4. We were also supposed to meet friends that night, but we missed each other and got a snotty note through our letter box instead!

Carol Darvill

True Love

From promotion in 1966 through to Champions in 1968, I had read every morning paper from back to front, gleaning all the glorious details, at 7 a.m. on the paper round. Even in Ladybarn, we had 'quality' papers to deliver, and they always had a report on City's games then. Now the *Manchester Guardian* doesn't bother with the Blue's midweek games unless there is a special angle, so don't buy it! Stick to the *Telegraph* and ignore the political pages. My elder sister covered the evening round, so that I didn't forego the Saturday afternoon games. At my school in Rusholme, the library always had all the broadsheets, so if I missed anything, that was where I spent lunchtime catching up. Mind you, so did half of my class, as the Blues had plenty of support from those who could pass the entrance exam! But having failed half of my 'O' levels (I wonder why?), my parents told me to get a proper Saturday job now I was sixteen if I wanted to go into the sixth form, and Tesco in Withington was in walking distance. I fooled myself that there were a lot of midweek games anyway, and my 66-match continuous run came to an end. How did I get through that winter? Well, seventeen-year-old Marilyn in miniskirts helped; as I was introduced to girls with legs that mother would disapprove of. We spent many a happy hour or two re-filling shelves and running upstairs to the stockroom, Friday night and all day Saturday. She was the first girl I dated; well I called it a date, sharing a warmed-up pie in the backroom. And we had a celebrity in our midst! This small Tesco, opposite The Albert, had about six staff and one of the checkout assistants, a mature twenty-one-year-old, was a cousin of Stan Bowles. Also, nearly opposite the shop was a Granada or Rumbelows TV rental shop, hence that was where I spent the last hour, nose pressed to the glass watching the teleprinter, and waiting for the league tables to flash up. I lost count of all the times I got hauled back over the road to fetch a ton of sugar or Daz downstairs. But the crunch came after the second successful season in a row. We had won the cup in 1969, and I had enough money to follow most of the Cup run, which included a few attempts at trying to find Blackburn's ground from Bury, reaching that shed of a stadium at 8.25 p.m. after crossing railway and canal down 'The Hill', later to become famous in the year 2000 promotion decider. It was still August, the sun was out, Marilyn (affectionately known as Mal) looked fantastic, and I had missed a couple of games already. Mal said she fancied it, the thing I was always going on about. I fell off my chair, in deep shock. She really wanted to go and watch City on a Saturday afternoon? I was in heaven, I thought. We were playing Everton, so a good game was anticipated. And I was taking a pretty girl for the first time! Just the one snag: we should both be working. One o'clock passed, then half past, then 1.45. We made a run for it and no one spotted us. Down Davenport Avenue, past Mal's house, across the park and along Yew Tree Road, with the ground in view and the crowd gathering. A big match, but loads of room on the Kippax, standing in the middle as usual, and hoping to see a few schoolmates to show off the 'bird'. No chance. Just when you want them they are nowhere to be seen. Needless to say, I didn't take much notice of the match, but Mal didn't take much notice of me either. A 1-1 draw, I think, and we raced back to work thinking we would get away with it. We didn't. Called into the office, we were both sacked and sent on our way. Typically, a week later Mal had her job back, and a big bruising twenty-one-year-old boyfriend, and I was banished from her memory. My Dad told me to get a job, but the only work was as a waiter at the Ladybarn British Legion, and I took it though I was underage. That was a good lesson too: never serve the public, and my future work was better defined because of it. Into the winter of 'A' levels, and it was a cold day to go to Wembley for the League Cup Final. My mates at school decided to travel by train and avoid going with a dad, as we had last year. We must have been growing up. (Incidentally, my first experience of seeing Wembley Way was fighting with Spurs fans, when we were playing Leicester.) We went into Soho, and on Poland Street found a café for the pre-match meal. I was shivering still from the train journey, which had been shocking, zero degrees outside and no heating inside. Ordered gammon, egg and chips and threw sugar all over it thinking it was salt, then sank three pints and headed for the ground. I was in pain, stomach all knotted up by now and it wasn't because of nerves. I could hardly stand up as we found our enclosures and did all the usual nipping in and out with ticket stubs until we were all in the same one. I thought I wanted the bogs but couldn't move, and couldn't stand up enough to see over the crowd. I had to keep going out of the enclosure and when the game kicked off, I stayed out on the stairs at the very top, peeping in occasionally for a glimpse of the action. The last thing I wanted was extra time! But we got it and it was hell! Still cold, of course, and an exciting game I'm told, with Doyle and Pardoe the scorers. I don't know who felt worse at the end, me or Buzzer with his fractured leg. Back to Euston, and I was barely able to walk, listening to the animated conversation of the successful trip to Wembley and feeling as though I hadn't been there. 7 March is too early and too cold for a final.

John Geary

CHAPTER 3

Man City Players

Goal ace Quinn saves a penalty

DISGRACED Manchester City goalkeeper Tony Coton faces a possible six match ban following a sending off and a reckless glove throwing incident at the referee in an explosive Maine Road match.

Coton was given the red card when he pulled down Derby County's Welsh international striker Dean Saunders in a fateful 33rd minute that led to the virtually doomed visitors being additionally awarded a penalty.

Before that could be taken the angry Coton hurled his gloves at Stockton referee Ken Lupton who called the player back to take a further note in his book which could mean an FA disrepute charge on top of the three match ban for the dismissal.

Niall Quinn, City's hero at one end with his 21st minute goal — his 20th of the season — which gave his side the lead then earned even greater applause when he superbly swooped to his left to save the spot kick from Saunders.

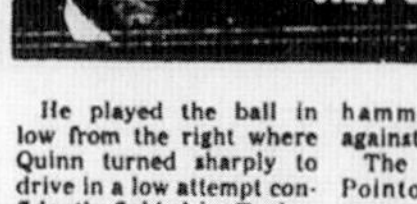

City foolishly allowed themselves to become involved, especially in the period after the sending off when the tackles were wild.

Booked

Additionally Mark Ward was booked for dissent as City battled to stretch their recent unbeaten run to six matches.

Hendry, fully recovered from a virus infection that forced him to spend a spell in hospital, returned after a six-match absence to take over from the injured Brightwell as an impressive replacement in the centre of the back four.

And it was Hendry, in an advanced position, who set up the Blues' first major threat.

He played the ball in low from the right where Quinn turned sharply to drive in a low attempt confidently fielded by Taylor, again substituting for ham string victim Peter Shilton.

Quinn started and almost finished another useful looking build-up. This time the big Irishman found Pointon and then took the return cross from the left back with a powerful header that was well held by Taylor.

Pointon was tripped from behind by Paul Williams, only for Heath to hammer the free kick against the defensive wall.

The ball broke loose to Pointon but his return cross was headed clear by Wilson.

Heath shot wide and then had an angled attempt from the right deflected for a corner as City pressure mounted against a Derby side on the brink of relegation.

And the drop to the Second Division looked even more ominous in the 21st minute when City finally found the target to race in to a 21st minute lead.

The ball bobbed tantalisingly across the fae of the Derby goal before Ward got up to head the ball back for QUINN to rifle in a vicious low effort that gave Taylor no chance.

County replied with Saunders crossing from the right and Hendry flinging himself full length to clear.

Saunders revealed a class that makes him a multi million pound striker when he went past two defenders to finish with a crisp low shot that Coton took at the second attempt. But then both players were to feature in a further and even more explosive incident.

Saunders beat the City off side trap and the Welsh marksman had cut in on goal, went round Coton but was then blatantly pulled down by the City goalkeeper.

The referee had no option but to send off Coton although the City goalkeeper foolishly did himself no favours by throwing his gloves at the official.

And the drama didn't end there either. Quinn took over the green jersey, and City's hero at one end earned equal acclaim at the other when he superbly flung himself to his left to beat out the penalty by Saunders and earn a standing ovation from the fans.

Yet City then allowed themselves to become even more involved and Ward was given the yellow card as other players flung themselves recklessly into challenges in a match now full of power and fury.

Wilson was injured in one of those challenges and he limped off to be replaced by Patterson after 40 mins.

Brave

White cut through on the almost identical course Saunders had taken when Coton pulled him down for the penalty, but this time Taylor bravely saved at the feet of the City striker.

Hill's excellent cross from the right found the head of Brennan whose splendid effort dipped over the bar by a matter of inches.

Forced to battle on with only ten men for the second time this season — Pointon was sent off at Queens Park Rangers in early March — City began to soak up more pressure.

Continued on Back Page

THE TEAMS

MAN CITY		DERBY
Coton	1	Taylor
Hill	2	Sage
Pointon	3	Pickering
Heath	4	G Williams
Hendry	5	Wright
Redmond	6	Kavanagh
White	7	Micklewhite
Brennan	8	Saunders
Quinn	9	Harford
Harper	10	Wilson
Ward	11	P Williams
Subs:		Subs:
Reid		Patterson
Allen		Cross

Referee: Ken Lupton, Stockton

Niall Quinn could have achieved sporting fame in a number of sports, including hurling and Gaelic football, but instead chose football. He was voted City' s Player of the Year for the season of 1990/91.

Who are the Man City favourites ... and why?

Being a City fan from 1980 and having missed out on the halcyon days of Bell, Lee and Summerbee *et al*, there has been little to cheer and no trophies to celebrate. The most successful spell within this period in the club's history was during Peter Reid's tenure, as he took the foundations of Howard Kendall's team and built upon it to produce a reasonably-skilled, hard-working side, who finished fifth, fifth and ninth respectively between 1991 and 1993. The focal point of that largely unsung City side was the towering 6ft 3in centre forward, Niall Quinn, who was arguably City's most influential player at that time. However, his arrival at Maine Road was not greeted with universal enthusiasm. In fact, this particular City fan was a little disappointed when he signed! City were heading towards safety in the old First Division in 1989/90, as Howard Kendall was building a solid, if unspectacular side, and he was in the market for a striker. Press reports suggested that City were supposedly in competition with ambitious Second Division Leeds United for Quinn's services, and I remember hoping that he would go to Leeds! After all, from what I'd seen, this awkward, gangling young Irishman appeared to be merely a target man, whom Arsenal brought on as a substitute when they were desperate to win a game, and he didn't appear to be a particularly good finisher or have a very good first touch. Put another way, prior to Quinn joining City, I thought that he was a donkey! So you can imagine that I was rather underwhelmed when Kendall signed him from Arsenal for £800,000 on 15 March 1990. How wrong I was! I am happy to say Quinn quickly won me over, along with any other doubter amongst the City fans, on his debut against Chelsea on 23 March 1990. He had already shown a good touch, and had linked up play well in a busy start, which saw Chelsea take the lead. Receiving the ball on the half-way line, he chested it down neatly and drove a long pass out to the right wing to David White, who sped down the wing. The long-striding Quinn bounded down the centre to meet White's accurate, low cross and drove it into the net sweetly and accurately from close range for City's equalizer. It was a goal of beautiful simplicity and a moment of real joy. In my joy, I was happy to be eating humble pie in being proved wrong! Quinn then gave six years' sterling service to the Blues, and was very much the focal point of the City attack. He bagged 20 goals in 1990/91, as City stormed to fifth place – a feat that had not been achieved by a City striker in the top flight since Brian Kidd in 1976/77. His link-up play was a vital part of Kendall's and Reid's workmanlike sides, which threatened to challenge for honours without quite making it. His control brought other players into the game and his flick-ons were capitalized on by other City players, none more so than winger-cum-striker David White. Indeed, City came to rely on Quinn a little too much, with the long ball to him being a rather over-used option at times – a tactic which opponents started to get used to in the later part of his City career. Nevertheless, we certainly looked lost without him. It was not just in attack that Niall Quinn's qualities shone through. Quinn was an archetypal team player, who was eager to help out his defence, his aerial ability digging City out of some tight situations on several occasions. All these qualities earned him the respect of every City player and every fan. It is not just the Quinn actions as a player that makes him my favourite City player, but

Quinn the man. A modest, level-headed, man, he always spoke eloquently of City, and his heart-felt disappointment at our relegation from the Premiership in 1996 was palpable. From a footballing point of view, it was curious that he was sold on as a cost-cutting measure in the summer of 1996, especially as we needed his battling qualities in the Nationwide League, but, unfortunately, Francis Lee's purge of the highest earners at City meant that Sunderland fans were to enjoy Quinn's talents rather than City fans. Once again under the managership of Peter Reid, he has gone on to form a deadly partnership with the prolific Kevin Phillips, which has seen the Wearsiders establish themselves as a Premiership side on the fringes of Europe – a further testament to his ability, and evidence that we really should have kept hold of him at City. Quinn always has the respect of the City faithful, and he is always guaranteed a warm ovation whenever the Blues play Sunderland: the appreciation of a fine Manchester City player, and a favourite.

Phil Banerjee

Uwe Rosler is my all-time favourite, no question, probably because most of my exposure to the team has been in the past ten or so years – thanks to the internet and the boom of TV highlights in the US and around the world. I loved Kinkladze, of course, but Uwe's passion won me over. He scored goals and he loved City. Summerbee is another favourite – although I saw him in *Escape to Victory* before I ever saw him in City colours. Also love Peter Barnes, Joe Royle, Niall Quinn and media mate Paul Hince.

Marc Stein

I do not really have an all-time favourite. I only saw Colin Bell in the twilight of his career, but Trevor Francis always sticks in my mind, especially after his debut away at Stoke City when he scored twice. Uwe Rosler was a revelation and Gio Kinkladze was a class player, but not a team player, and I am too young to remember Bert Trautmann and any other greats from that era or earlier.

Nick Walker

Dennis Tueart. Well, mainly because he was the main striker for me during my first years as a supporter. Of course I had other favourite players, like, obviously, Colin Bell, but also big Joe Corrigan and Peter Barnes. Dennis Tueart also seemed to be a very honest and down-to-earth type of person, who had a lot of time for the supporters and had a passion or bond with the club which has obviously manifested itself in the present position I am pleased to see him in. He seems spiritually connected to Manchester City, just as the rest of us are. (Pass my medication please, love!) The goal he scored at Wembley in February 1976 simply reinforced his standing in my eyes. He was definitely a hero after that superb memorable moment from City's history, which, regrettably, was the last 'real' silverware for the club. I am so pleased that I was at Wembley that day against a Newcastle United side managed by Gordon Lee (and his black and white army) and with the likes of Alan Gowling (who scored for Newcastle) and Malcolm 'Super Mac' Macdonald in the side. Our team were heroes, and I stood on the terracing with the blue and white army of Tony Book's era, singing my little heart out along with the other members of the Openshaw branch of the City supporters' club whom I had travelled with. I was then, without doubt, 'City 'til I die'. Tueart's goal was simply breathtaking, and we erupted. It was from a floating cross by Willie Donachie, after a run on the left which was headed back to near the penalty spot by Tommy Booth, and sheer acrobatics from Dennis Tueart made the score 2-1. What a truly memorable goal, which was his twentieth of the season, I think. Joe Royle had a goal disallowed not long after. Europe beckoned! 'Ian McFarlane' was the chant at the end, when even Helen Turner (ring my bell) joined the lap of honour. I reckon that Paul Dickov could reach similar long-term cult status after his goal at Wembley (apologies to super Kevin Horlock, whose goal was just as vital), but Paul's effort and commitment is plain to see for me, and I hope he always has some form of connection with us.

Mark Redgrave

A masterly, complete footballer, described as the best-ever player produced by Ireland, and considered by many experts to be the best-ever British footballer. He figures in the Football League's '100 Legends' and was nominated by the Post Office for their Football Legends stamps issue. Peter Doherty is City's greatest ever player.

Mark Edwards

Left: *Dennis Tueart was a very honest and down-to-earth type of person, who had a lot of time for the supporters.* Right: *Gio Kinkladze is one of the greatest entertainers to grace Maine Road in recent years.*

Left: *Peter Doherty is represented here by one of a series of fifty cigarette cards, which were produced by W.D. & H.O. Wills.* Right: *Roy Paul – one of the greatest wing-halves of his day.*

My number one City player is the peerless Peter Doherty; the greatest inside forward ever.

Andrew Thomas

If he is not considered by many City fans to be the best player, Roy Paul must at least be the best half-back.

Trevor Bowring

Rodney Marsh is my all-time favourite. At the time, we were a real workman-like team, really successful. He was the icing on the cake, and he did United every game. Rodney was fantastic against United, he came alive. I was ecstatic when we signed him because I loved him when he was at QPR. I loved that sort of player, that's what City players should be about. Unfortunately, we have no one like that at the moment. Trevor Francis was probably the most talented player I have seen at City, unbelievable pace, unbelievable finishing. What a pity we only got twenty-odd games out of him.

Tom Ritchie

Definitely Georgi Kinkladze, for his brilliant skill on the ball.

Noel Bayley

Manchester City has produced some wonderful footballers through its ranks down the years. Paul Lake was one such player. It is because of his exceptional ability, the fact that he is also a true blue Manchester City supporter, and because he is a local lad of a similar age to me, that he is a favourite player of mine. Capable of playing in almost any position – anywhere across the back four or midfield, or even up front – the only position that he was never asked to play in light blue was goalkeeper, and he played each position like it was his own. Indeed, when asked to play in either full-back position, he filled it with no little skill. His best position was a matter of debate. Consensus suggested that his best position was centre-back, mainly due to his excellent reading of the game, and exceptional all-round ability. Whilst I believe that he would have been international class at centre-back, I beg to differ, having seen Lakey's above average skills employed in midfield, and ability to dribble and beat a man with either foot. I believe that a left-sided midfield role would have been his most effective position, and that those skills would have gone to waste had he been employed in defence. Playing in a 'tucked-in' left-sided role in the 5-1 thrashing of Manchester United in 1989, he had an inspired game to set up two goals. Lake was everywhere in defence and attack in an outstanding team performance. Another enduring image of that game was his clenched fist celebration and the expression of joy on his face when David Oldfield steered home the first goal – a kind of 'YEEEEEEEES' expression – which said how much it mattered to a local lad to be beating his local rivals. It was a feeling any City supporter can identify with, and is another reason why Paul Lake is a favourite. Two-footed, Paul had excellent control, and accurate passing skills, which made him equally comfortable in midfield as in defence, but Howard Kendall, who managed City between 1989 and 1990, decided that his best position was in central defence. Given the chance to fill one position consistently, Lake forced his way into Bobby Robson's squad of forty for the 1990 World Cup in Italy. Rumours in the press suggested that Liverpool had found the replacement for their own great central defender Alan Hansen, and were ready to make City an offer. It seemed like the world was at Paul Lake's feet. So, what a tragedy it was that his career was cut short by a horrific knee injury, which nowadays might well have been cured fully. The very premature end of Paul Lake's career is perhaps the biggest footballing tragedy that beset Manchester City in recent times. I've not had the pleasure of meeting

Rodney Marsh – a footballer and entertainer supreme.

Paul Lake, but when I think about it, I have to say that I still mourn it. Not only were City robbed of a potential great, but England also. Lake was a player that was ahead of his time. In his darkest moments, Paul may rue the fact that his career ended far too early, but he can still take some consolation at least. Paul Lake achieved what the vast majority of Manchester City supporters can only dream about: he has pulled on that blue Manchester City shirt and played for the first team ... and won a Manchester Derby.

Phil Banerjee

A wee Scot who made a lasting impression on me and lit up the autumn of 1983:

'Five foot eight,
Underweight,
Jimmy Tolmie's
F****n' great!'

Gary Stevens

The era I was brought up in evolved around Joe Corrigan. He used to save a lot of games for us. The most romantic player for City has got to be Colin Bell. Arguably the greatest player City could have had would be Paul Lake, but he got injured and never got the chance to fulfil his talent. I remember Malcolm Allison's comment: 'He was like an Austin Metro, but with a Rolls Royce engine'.

Seamus McAndrew

It's most definitely Dave Watson, a great centre half who went on to play for England. I

Jim Tolmie – one of Billy McNeill's many Scottish signings. Jim was formerly with Morton, but signed from Belgium club Lokeren.

will always remember one of the games he played in for England, when he laid out an Italian centre forward at Wembley.

Paul Mitchell

Joe Corrigan, he was a great goalkeeper. Underrated for his country with Shilton and Clemence in front of him, and, at the time, was a very tall for a goalkeeper. These days he would be like a dwarf.

Richard Purcell

I have several favourite players from over the years, but overall it has to be Colin Bell for his consistency, he seemed to have very few bad games. The best centre half City had was Dave Watson.

Steve Boyd

Colin Bell is my favourite player because there was no one better. He could pass the ball, he could run with the ball, he scored goals and was a top man.

Steve Massey

The best player I have seen in all the time I have been watching Manchester City is Willie Donachie. It was a shame when he left to go and play football in America for Portland Timbers. These days he is a very highly respected coach and will undoubtedly always remain one of my favourite players.

Tom Welch

One man who has always stood out is Ron Futcher and, without doubt, the highlight of his City career is a classic hat-trick he scored in a game at Chelsea. It was only the second game of what was to be a brief career at City, and one where he left the ground with the match ball and three stitches to a head wound. He scored his first goal on forty minutes, and the second when he finished a

Left: *In the 1970s, Joe Corrigan was the tallest goalkeeper in the League at 6ft 4.5in.* Right: *In many people's eyes, Dave Watson was the best centre half City ever had. He signed from Sunderland for £275,000 in June 1975.*

move started by his brother, Paul, on forty-four minutes. He completed his hat-trick with a diving header in the second half.

Daniel Thomas

Both Colin Bell who, with Franny Lee, started me off following City, and Gio Kinladze – immense skill, shame it wasn't used to its full ability. Currently has to be Dicky for his total dedication to the cause, and also Danny Tiatto, 'cos I just love the way he mixes it and tries to look innocent afterwards!

Carol Darvill

As a schoolboy, Dennis Tueart was my all-time hero, and just when I thought I was too old for heroes, Niall Quinn filled that position – not just for his on-the-pitch efforts, but also for his off-the-pitch activities. At the time when certain players from a certain team in Manchester sought publicity by attending all the right nightclubs and restaurants, Niall Quinn was attending picket lines outside a hostel in Ardwick for the homeless, in support of better conditions for workers and residents. To his great credit, he did this without seeking any publicity or glory. I will also never forget the game in which he both scored a goal *and* saved a penalty against Derby County.

Phill Gatenby

I think players from your formative years (until about eighteen-ish) are the ones who impress the most, and stay with you forever. I realised, at the age of eleven years old, that

Willie Donachie was a consistent full-back, who represented Scotland at international level. He is currently head coach at Sheffield Wednesday.

I'd have to be a goalie, as I was totally useless as an outfield player. Stranded between two piles of coats on a bombsite in a twenty-a-side game, I made one stupendous save, which I knew nothing about. My 'style' was to march up and down between the 'goal-posts', and whilst performing this frenzied sentry duty, the local star whacked in a shot which caught my left knee in ascendancy, and the ball flew off down the pitch apace, much to everyone's delight and amusement. From then on, I made the position my own. City had just reached Wembley (and beaten United three times in the season) with the best goalkeeper around, Bert Trautmann, so

Left: *Trevor Francis was once described by then City manager John Bond as being 'the biggest personality to hit Manchester, since George Best was at his peak'.* Right: *Colin Bell joined Man City during the 1955/56 season from Bury. He is widely considered to be one of the greatest footballers ever to play for City, and was an integral part of the First Division Championship-winning side of 1967/68. He also achieved international honours with England.*

I became a Blue, and Favourite player has to be Colin Bell; he was so like me as a player! A strong runner, up and down the pitch, tackles in both boxes, shoots clinically, headers fly in, and tactically, always naturally in position. I've never seen anybody like it since in a blue shirt.

John Geary

Bert was my role model and hero. I'm afraid I failed him badly! It was his heroics in the mid-1950s cup runs and bravery in the 1956 cup final which clinched it for me with City, though the sky blue had something to do with it too. Outfield, I loved Paddy Fagan's brilliant wing play; Dave Ewing, Bill Leivers and Roy Paul for their toughness and character; Joe Hayes for his goals, Colin Barlow for his speed, Cliff Sear's sliding tackles, and Bobby Johnstone for his skill. The *whole* of the 1968 team were wonderful, as was Trevor Francis, briefly, Tueart and Barnes (father *and* son), and, of course, Gio Kinkaldze, the magician, who is a modern-day Bobby J.

Dave Wallace

CHAPTER 4

The Goals

Manchester City v. Manchester United, 11 February 1996. Uwe Rosler lobs the ball over the outstretched arms of Peter Schmeichel to give City the lead in the FA Cup.

Everyone has a favourite goal, be it the most significant or the most memorable or maybe even the funniest ...

Both of mine, unfortunately, came in defeat – both from Uwe, both against United in the 1995/96 season. Uwe chipped us into a lead over Schmeichel in the FA Cup tie that was ultimately ruined by the horrible decision against Frontzeck. I watched it in a pub with ex-pats in Los Angeles, almost all of them United fans. When Uwe scored, the few City fans in the pub rushed the big screen and started hugging each other like we were part of the celebration on the field. It was pretty hilarious. The other was Uwe's blistering run and strike against United later that season. We were 2-1 down when he came on, having been dropped for Kavelashvili. He slammed the ball through Steve Bruce's legs, and then trampled Nigel Clough in the post-goal celebration, so he could point at his name and point at Alan Ball. I still pull the tapes out to watch those babies.

Marc Stein

Paul Dickov's goal at Wembley for its importance. I was there and was all set to go after the second goal went in for Gillingham, and put my jacket on ready to go. Then Horlock scored and then when Dickov scored, I could not believe it. I was crying with joy and saw Dante Friend along my row who was exactly the same. Thus, I decided to keep my jacket on for luck through extra time and penalties. It worked, but I was boiling hot.

Philip Noble

Paul Dickov fires in City's injury-time equalizer against Gillingham, 30 May 1999.

There are a couple of contenders for most significant in recent years: obviously Dickov against Gillingham or Goater against Blackburn, Goater against Wigan, Taylor against Birmingham, but my personal choice might have to be Gareth Taylor against Stoke, when the whole direction of the club turned round in 'that' second half. I think everyone came away knowing they had witnessed something pretty momentous that day. Most memorable might have to be Mike Sheron *v.* Spurs in the FA Cup quarter-final because City fans being City fans, the early goal confirmed what we already believed, our name was on the cup that year, except it obviously wasn't. Still, the actual moment was nice. As for funniest, I'd have to say Dickov's against Millwall. With the recent history building events up, the game was looking like it had 0-0 written all over it, then Spink lets a pea-roller trickle between his legs late on, and the Millwall fans start a riot and try to destroy the ground! Their reactions were every bit as hilarious as Spink's!

Mike Holden

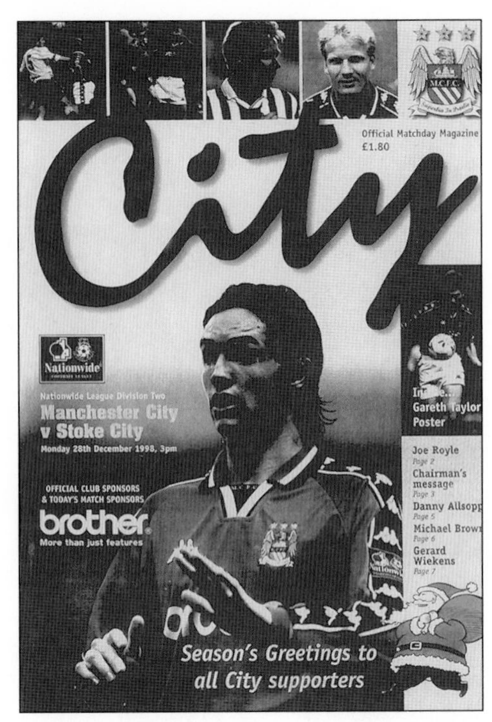

A programme from the game against Stoke City, 28 December 1998. Gareth Taylor's goal was the turning point for City's fortunes in the 1998/99 season.

I have seen many great goals that stick in your mind. Jim Melrose against Notts. County from the halfway line, Clive Allen at Chelsea, Kinkladze against Southampton, Steve Mackenzie in the FA Cup Final against Tottenham Hotspur – the list is endless. A wee curly-haired Scotsman by the name of Jim Tolmie scored one special goal, and here's the reason why. At the time, the City match magazine ran a golden goal competition, where a unique time in seconds was printed in every programme, and if your time matched the time of the first goal scored in the game, you won £50. The game was back in the early 1980s. A League Cup game, I think, and City were playing Torquay. A penalty was awarded to City early on in the game, Tolmie stepped up and converted it and yes, you have guessed right. The time of the goal matched the time in my programme, and City won the game 6-0.

Andrew Thomas

The best goal, without a doubt, has to be when Jim Melrose let fly from just over the halfway line at home against Notts County on 8 December 1984.

Gary Stevens

A programme from the Milk Cup second round match, which shows 'Golden Goal' hero, Jim Tolmie, 25 October 1983.

We do not get to Wembley very often, but when we do it's normally quite memorable, and as goals go, Steve Mackenzie's drive from thirty yards has to be my most memorable. Somehow, in the national press, it was overshadowed by Ricky Villa's goal.

Tony Morgans

Kinkladze against Southampton, the run and chip over Beasant. It was a wonder goal.

Peter O'Brien

I remember the time back in 1989 when we beat United 5-1. All five of the goals were memorable for one reason or another, but I suppose the fifth and last goal will always stick in my mind. Bishop passed the ball out to David White on the right wing and Hinchcliffe met his cross perfectly at the far post. Absolute pandemonium broke out in all the stands, and the faces of the United supporters – what a picture.

Chris Boyd

My favourite goal has to be one of Dave Watson's. It was a header from about twenty-five yards out against Ipswich Town; we won 2-1 in the 1976/77 season. Goals from recent times would have to include Kinkladze against Southampton and one from Mark

Kennedy – two seasons ago against Bolton, when he ran from the halfway line and sent in a dipping shot.

Steve Boyd

My most memorable goal has to be Paul Dickov's equalizer against Gillingham, that was superb – it was a dream moment – and then the penalty shoot-out, when people who couldn't bear to look all looked at me, rather than face the goal!

Seamus McAndrew

I will always remember a goal from the 'king', Colin Bell. It was at Chelsea in the FA Cup in front of 50,000 people back in the 1970s. He volleyed the ball home from the right-hand side of the box, just on the edge of it, and it was at the Shed End.

Tom Finneran

Jim Melrose at Maine Road against Notts County. He was barely over the halfway line when he fired this one in.

Jackie Coyle

It's a goal from Barry Silkman for me, away at Ipswich Town in the March of 1979. He hit it from just in front of the halfway line.

Brian Hince

Thinking about goals in derby games, I recall a real peach of a goal from Ian Brightwell at Old Trafford in 1990. It was a brilliant goal: minutes earlier, United had scored, but this was a goal as soon as it left his foot, he let fly with a shot from about thirty to thirty-five yards out. You will not see a better goal than that in a derby game for some time.

Nick Walker

My goal was not so much a brilliant one but a vital one, in a similar vein to Dickov's goal against Gillingham at Wembley in the play-off final. The goal was scored against Bradford City at their ground, we had battered them all day and various scores were coming in from other important games, but we just needed a point from the game to be

A programme from the game when Jim Melrose scored his spectacular goal from the halfway line against Notts County, 8 December 1984.

Tueart's goal against Newcastle, 28 February 1976. Dennis Tueart's spectacular goal restored City's lead in the 1976 League Cup Final against Newcastle United, and is a memory that will stay with those who saw it for a long time.

promoted, we were desperate for a goal and Trevor Morley supplied it at the end, where all the City fans were housed.

Julie Clark

Certainly one of the greatest goals ever scored at Wembley has to be Dennis Tueart's against Newcastle United in 1976. Tueart was genuinely world-class and, of course, we won the cup.

Steve Green

I went to a game once – away at Ipswich, on the train – back in the late 1970s. For some reason, we got to the game late (leaves on the line) and saw Barry Silkman score a goal for City, he must have been at least forty-five to fifty yards out.

Craig James

Clive Allen, in a game at Chelsea. The Chelsea players were appealing for a free-kick, but Clive just hit the ball on the volley from twenty-five yards out, and it just flew into the net.

Adam Dowell

Two goals from Trevor Francis on his debut away at Stoke in September 1981 are memorable for me. It was not just the quality of the goals, but the whole day itself. There were thousands of us there that day, packed in like sardines, and there was a real buzz in the air.

Chris Cronin

A lob from inside the centre circle by Jim Melrose is, without a doubt, one of the most spectacular goals I have ever seen at Maine Road. It was against Notts County.

Mike Byrne

In a game at Maine Road against Tottenham, when the new Umbro Stand, as it was at the time, was opened. Terry Phelan scored a consolation goal for City in an FA Cup match against Tottenham. Phelan always reminded me of a ferret darting about everywhere, and this goal was great – he ran for miles with the ball to score, and sparked an ugly pitch invasion.

Phil Rowe

A goal from David White against Liverpool in 1991 was debated for days after, even resulting in a phone poll on Granada TV by Elton Welsby, as to whether it crossed the line or not. Course it did!

Brad Hamlin

What about some greatest goals, but with a slightly different side to them? Own goals!

Mackenzie's goal against Tottenham, 14 May 1981. Steve Mackenzie volleys home a spectacular drive against Tottenham in the replay of the 100th FA Cup Final. Tottenham eventually ran out 3-2 winners.

A programme from the home game against Ipswich, 2 April 1977, when Dave Watson scored with a header from twenty-five yards out.

Here are some that spring to mind right away:
– Tommy Hutchison *v.* Tottenham in the FA Cup Final in May 1981. I don't think I need to say much about this one.
– Jamie Pollock, at home to QPR in April 1998. What a costly own goal and, if I remember rightly, he became an instant hero with the subscribers to some QPR fanzine.
– This one, I think, was live on TV, which makes it even worse. It came in an away game at Wolves in April 1998, and Martyn Margetson somehow managed to drop a corner kick through his legs.
– Colin Hendry scored an own goal in a derby match at Old Trafford in May 1991, but everybody claimed (except us City fans) it was a goal to Ryan Giggs, making his debut for United.

Neil Hughes

Not one, but several memorable goals:
– Denis Law, against Manchester United back in April 1974.
– The first of the famous five against United by David Oldfield, just to see Gary Pallister miss the ball at full stretch.
– Paul Power, against Ipswich in the FA Cup semi-final at Villa Park. What a goal that was!
– A goal by Paul Lake at Blackpool in the FA Cup. There was an almighty free-for-all in the Blackpool penalty box, before Lakey lashed it home and brought City back into the game.
– Another goal against United, this time by Ian Brightwell. He hit the ball with such conviction, it just flew in.

Eric Walsh

In no particular order – my first favourite would have to be the FA Cup semi-final winner *v.* Ipswich in 1981. It was the week before we got married, and I still got moaned at for getting home late! Second favourite would be David White's hat-trick goal in the 10-1 victory over Huddersfield Town. Third favourite is Andy Hinchcliffe's stonking header against United in the 5-1 derby drubbing. Fourth favourite – Gio's goal against Southampton, sheer class. Lastly, Dicky's equalizer in the play-offs at Wembley – I still get tearful every time I see it!

Carol Darvill

Of course, Gio's goal against Southampton will last in the memory forever, but I also recall a goal by Tueart at Stoke City in the late 1970s. Tueart ran at the defence from the halfway line, ghosting past four defenders effortlessly, before smashing the ball at Peter Shilton – who could only parry the ball back to Tueart who followed up by putting the ball in the back of the net! Unfortunately, as with many games then, it was not recorded on TV. Paul Dickov's equaliser at Wembley too, still brings tears to the eye every time I watch it.

Phill Gatenby

So many. Surprisingly, Jim Melrose against Notts County in 1984/85 stands out the most. If I remember right, Jim took the ball on his thigh, just over the halfway line, close to the Kippax. In one movement, he turned and lofted the ball goalwards towards the North Stand end, catching County 'keeper Jim McDonagh unawares and off his line, as it sailed into the net. There was Dennis Tueart's overhead and Dave Watson's header in 1977 *v.* Ipswich, Denis Law's third at Luton in 1960/61, and hmmmm, yes, 'that' back-heel in 1974. Tony Book's bouncing bomb at home to break the deadlock against Everton in 1968, on the same night that West Brom beat United 6-3 to set us up for the final two games and the title; Tommy Booth's winner in the 1969 semi-final, and Paul Power's in 1981. Kinky's goals *v.* Southampton and Leicester in 1996, Paul Dickov's equalizer in the play-off final, Shaun Goater's equalizer at Blackburn, and Steve Howey's at Old Trafford wasn't bad. They all stand out.

Dave Wallace

My favourite goal at Maine Road is probably the Kinky goal against Southampton, but for many years, I swore that the best goal I'd seen was scored in a reserve fixture. I don't know what year it was, probably late 1970s, and I can't remember the opposition, but the goal was a volley by Mick Docherty, son of the former Reds manager, Tommy, which I swear was scored from the edge of the centre circle. Does anyone remember that goal?

Ian Cheeseman

The goal I recall that was special was featured on Match of the Day, in a FA cup match away at Chelsea in the early 1970s. I think Summerbee supplied a cross-field ball to Bell steaming in on the right, and he smacked it from the corner of the penalty area on the volley and it flew in, nearly breaking the net. A similar player has graced the Bridge recently, capable of very good goals, Gus

A programme from the First Division game against Ipswich, 31 March 1979, which is remembered by some for the goal scored by Barry Silkman.

Ian Brightwell celebrates his spectacular long-range strike against Manchester United, 3 February 1990.

Poyet, and I'd like to see him in a blue shirt too. I was there, at the opposite end of the dog track to the Shed, and happy to have made it into the ground safely, to worry later about how to get out again, always a problem at Stamford Bridge. I think we won 3-1 in the end, and I had met my pals in London, having travelled down on the special train. Straight after the game, we all quickly went our separate ways, and I headed for the tube, and suddenly realised I had no money left for the tube, I'd meant to ask my mates for a sub in the pub. Panicking, I started to run to Euston, thinking I could just get there for about 6.10 p.m. if I didn't stop (I was a cross-country runner at school, because there were too many good football players and I wanted to do a sport). After about twenty minutes, I was in Kensington and knackered and saw a bus going to Baker Street, so hopped on and jumped off as soon as the conductor came near. This got me just close enough to Euston to run the rest, and I caught the train with a few minutes to spare. Mind you, being broke in those days was nothing new, watching City every week, and I had perfected a way of travelling from London to Manchester on trains ticket-less, and made it a few times without getting caught. That's another story though.

John Geary

CHAPTER 5
Have you travelled miles to watch a match?

Left: *This is a programme from the Celtic game, when (reportedly) there were very few City fans in attendance.* Right: A *match programme from the game against Vilhelmina.*

The more weird and wonderful the stories you have, the better … in particular if you found the match in question had been called off altogether.

Earning My Stripes

I have been following City from afar since I was eleven years old. Visiting my family in Israel every summer, the only sports publication I found in English was *Shoot* magazine. I picked City because I loved their kit – back cover photo of the late, great Tommy Caton – and stuck with 'em ever since. Didn't get to see the Blues in person until 1996. Came to London from the US for a brief trip, with a subsequent stop in Manchester as well, but my first match was at Selhurst Park to watch the mighty Blues absorb a 3-1 hammering by Palace. It was our first season after relegation, and right around the time Dave Bassett was accepting and then refusing the manager's post. It was the first match I ever witnessed in England, and was floored by all the singing. At 3-0 down, City fans started singing 'Blue Moon', and didn't stop for a good half-hour. I swear they just kept singing and singing, out-working the team. I had goose bumps. Tears, almost. As a sports journalist in the States, I have covered almost every kind of professional sporting event you can imagine. I have covered the NBA for the past eight years, and all the other major leagues, along with the Olympics, World Cup, etc. In all that time, I have never witnessed a greater display of passion and unity and creativity as I did that day. I will never forget it. My next match was the 4-1 hammering at Lincoln in the League Cup, which some will say is the most embarrassing defeat the club has ever suffered. That allowed me to quickly earn my stripes from all the UK Blues, who assured me that I hadn't suffered nearly enough to really know the City experience. Doesn't get much worse than making your dream pilgrimage to Blue Heaven, bumming a ride from London to Lincoln, seeing your beloved Uwe Rosler score in the first two minutes to make it all even more of a tease, then watch the whole thing dissolve into the modern-day Halifax. That hurt me.

Marc Stein

Stand By Me

Well, two college mates and myself tried to hitch-hike to Norwich after the pub one Friday night, which seemed like a good idea at the time, but we only ended up as far as Hilton Park services on the M6. Why we chose to go down the M6 and not the A6, I don't know, but after a long night walking through the countryside towards Knutsford without any sleep, nothing really made any sense anymore! We were all a bit daft and didn't think much in those days, but our adventure reminded me a bit of the kids in the film *Stand By Me*, where they went walking for days and just spent the time taking the mickey out of each other. Needless to say, we gave up with Carrow Road still about 200 miles away and thumbed a lift back to Manchester at about 1 p.m. on the Saturday. City drew 1-1, with Fitzroy Simpson equalizing about two minutes from the end, and United beat Ipswich 9-0.

Mike Holden, Chips 'n' Gravy *fanzine*

Snow

The first time I travelled to watch City was probably when I went to see Celtic against Manchester City in a pre-season friendly in 1970. I was thirteen, and went on the train with my granddad, and there were about six City fans in a crowd of 70,000 at Hampden Park. The match finished 0-0, and Joe Corrigan got a guard of honour at the end for his performance on the night. Another game I remember is a game that was called off at Nottingham Forest in the cup in 1977. I travelled across the Peak District on my own in my car. The conditions were unbelievable, 2ft of snow, and when I got to the City

Ground, there was nobody there apart from two policemen on the main road. I went across to one of the coppers and asked him what had happened to the match, and he said it had been called off two hours ago. My radio had packed in, so I did not know. I travelled all the way back and then went the following Wednesday, this time on the coach, and we got beat 2-1.

Tom Ritchie

I Nutmegged Jason Beckford

During a pre-season tour of Sweden, City played a game in Lapland against a team called Vilhelmina IF. This has to be one of the remotest places where City have ever played a game. I went there with eleven other Blues. We got a bus from Skelleftea, which took four hours to reach Vilhelmina. Four hours of nothing but looking at trees. We caused the locals a lot of amusement when we all jumped up to look at a reindeer that had wandered onto the road (seeing a reindeer to the locals must be like seeing a cow in England). When we reached our destination, we booked into some lakeside cabins on a campsite on the edge of the town. There was only one bar in town, so naturally we ended up there at the night time. We met the goalkeeper who would be playing against City the following day in the bar and had a talk with him. The beer was very expensive, but thankfully we had some cans and wine back at the cabins. The following day, we had a couple of beers in the bar before the game and got some cans from the off-licence to take to the game. City played really well and ran out 7-0 winners after being two up at half-time. Notable achievements during the game were Mark Brennan's first goal for the club and a Clive Allen hat-trick. Both teams had a meal after the game in the Vilhelmina hotel – which just happened to be where we were, as it was the only bar in the town. We talked to a few of the City team, but they were staying some three hours away from Vilhelmina, so could not stay long. After the City team left, we ended up having a drink with their team. One bloke bought all the City fans a drink, which came to something like £50. We thought he was a nutter and we were right, as we found out afterwards he had once run amok through the town with a machete. We had a good old singsong with their team and taught them a few City songs, *Blue Moon* being one of their favourites. Once the bar shut, we invited their team and manager back to our log cabins. Their manager went home and brought back with him a big bottle of whisky and a bottle of Jack Daniels. We had a real good time talking to their players. A young midfielder was really pleased, because he had managed to nutmeg Jason Beckford. The beer and whisky flowed, and the party finished at about 4.30 a.m. It was a real good night. I've often had a good session with opposing fans, but never before with the opposing team and their manager.

Wilson Pratt

The Big Cheese

A noon pick-up at Aytoun Street on Tuesday 11 October 1988 was the latest chapter in a busy week in the history of Manchester City Football Club. Having already visited Portman Road the previous Saturday to witness a 1-0 defeat, only memorable for Bill William's one and only appearance, we were now off to Plymouth Argyle to try and defend a solitary one-goal lead in the second leg of

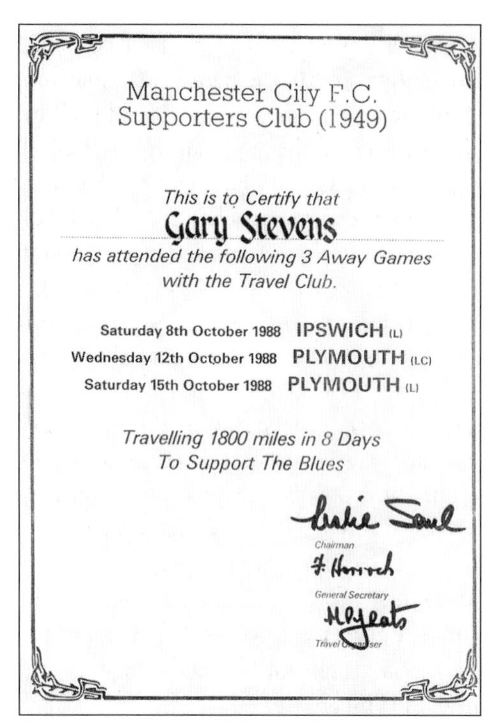
Manchester City F.C.
Supporters Club (1949)

This is to Certify that
Gary Stevens
has attended the following 3 Away Games with the Travel Club.

Saturday 8th October 1988 IPSWICH (L)
Wednesday 12th October 1988 PLYMOUTH (LC)
Saturday 15th October 1988 PLYMOUTH (L)

Travelling 1800 miles in 8 Days To Support The Blues

Chairman
General Secretary
Travel Organiser

A certificate awarded to fans who had covered 1,800 miles in eight days to support their team.

a Littlewoods Cup second round tie, or so we thought. It had started raining by the time we hit the M5, and as we approached Taunton at about 4.30 p.m., most of the passengers on Finglands coach 'B' had dropped off. The driver had BBC Radio Devon on, and I can still remember hearing the news that tonight's cup game at Home Park had been postponed due to a waterlogged pitch. Everyone suddenly woke up and began coming to terms with this bombshell news. Both coaches pulled off the motorway onto Taunton Deane services to decide our next move. Inevitably, the decision was made to turn round at the next junction and head back to Manchester. I could scarcely believe that Plymouth had called the game off just three hours before kick-off, and with us at least three-quarters of the way there. I arrived back at Bury train station, as it was then, and bumped straight into a mob of Everton supporters coming away from their cup game at Gigg Lane. I can't remember exactly when I found out that our game had been re-arranged for the following night. So, it was off again to Aytoun Town Street on the Wednesday morning for the return journey. This time, only one coach made the trip, and I think the £10 fare was either halved or waived altogether. This time the game did go ahead, and what a memorable one it turned out to be, City coming out on top with a Nigel Gleghorn-inspired 6-3 win. The team had probably travelled straight from Suffolk down to the South West because, as often happens with cup draws, a quirk of the fixture list had City playing at Plymouth again on the Saturday in a Second Division match. I am sure that this was the reason that the cup tie was re-arranged at such short notice, because the team was staying down there in a Devon hotel any way. No such luxuries for us supporters, as I had to put in an appearance at work on Thursday and get down to Maine Road to see the reserves draw 2-2 with Everton Reserves on the Thursday night. It was a familiar journey on the Saturday, and this time a Brian Gayle goal was enough to collect all three points. A few even stopped on another night to see City lift the Keith Soloman Memorial Shield, with a 6-2 win at Truro City on the Sunday. Two months later, we were invited into the Blue Room beneath the Maine Stand, prior to the home game with Shrewsbury Town, to meet the big cheese himself, P.J. Swales – all Cuban heels and comb-over – to receive our certificates. '1,800 miles in 8 days to support the Blues', it stated. The truth was nearer 2,250 miles, what with the wasted trip on the Tuesday!

Gary Stevens

Three And A Bit

As for travelling long distances, well it's just par for the course. The worst week I can remember was travelling to Ipswich on a Saturday, and then Plymouth on Tuesday, only to be told when we reached Taunton that the game was off, postponed till the following night! Same journey again on the Wednesday, having made use of my extra day off to recover from the original trip! On the Saturday, we were at Plymouth again, this time in the league! Peter Swales (City chairman at that time) gave all those who attended those 'three and a bit' marathon journeys in a week on the Supporters' Club coach, a special certificate.

Ian Cheeseman

Jack Frost

That has to be the time when I was a steward with City's travel club. There were three times when I went on the train to Aston Villa, we were not very lucky with that. Luck also favoured me when I did not go to Plymouth, that's the game when everybody got to Taunton. The furthest I have been, and then it was called off on the night, is Brentford, when it suddenly became frosty, especially after everything had been alright during the afternoon.

Steve Boyd

The Mummy

Travelling miles for a postponed game lit the blue touch paper in the memory box of a trip I undertook on Easter Saturday 1965 to urge Manchester City on into the First Division, hopefully, at the expense of Charlton Athletic at The Valley. Hopes held high by the signing of the fabulous Colin Bell, I signed on at a local newsagent in Didsbury, M20, to board the coach run by Finglands early on Saturday morning, 9 April 1966. I presented myself at the appointed time at the picking up spot, and was more and more aware as the minutes ticked by that there was a distinct lack of blue and white scarves amongst the early morning shoppers near me, much less a queue. Suddenly a Jag pulled up at the kerb, the driver leaned over and wound down the window, and spoke. Ever mindful even then of my mother's warnings about getting into strange cars with even stranger men, I nervously shuffled backwards up the pavement until what he was saying filtered through.

' ... I said, are you the bloke who booked at Bradley's to go to Charlton with Finglands?'
'Er, yes ... '
'Well everyone knew each other and decided to go at midnight. Nobody knew how to get in touch with you, so they asked me to save you a seat on one of my coaches.'

Within seconds I was aboard the Jag, and moving briskly towards Ashton-Under-Lyne, the headquarters of Mayne's. I settled down on my unexpected steed, opened my paperback (and probably my sandwiches for lunch) and off we went. Everything was going smoothly. Alright, so it was chucking it down on the M1 in the North Midlands, but so what. We were unbeaten in the last 14 League games and what could stop us picking up another two promotion points in London? The answer to that question was provided by the coach radio somewhere around Luton: ' ... and here is the list of the games postponed today up to now … (blah blah blah) … and Charlton Athletic against Manchester City'. We settled back glumly in our seats and peered out at the sodden countryside through the misted windows. Then we noticed we were turning into a slip road leading to a service area. The driver turned off the engine, stood, and shouted 'Right, have you lot decided which match you wanna see instead?' Hands groped under the seats for discarded tabloids, fixture lists were scanned and unanimously, the verdict was Chelsea *v.* West Ham at Stamford Bridge. Off we went again, while we desperately tried to remember who played for which side, how we'd gone on against each other that season, when I became aware of an elderly figure brushing past me towards the driver. We'd noticed this elderly couple at the rear of the coach earlier and had wondered at their fanaticism, travelling to watch the Blues at their age. Seated as I was at the front, I was privileged to overhear the entire conversation between the elderly supporter and the driver.

'What time do we get to Charlton?' asked the passenger.
'We're not going to Charlton, it's off, the lads want to go to Chelsea.'
'But me and the wife are going to Charlton.'
'I've told you, the match is off at Charlton, and we are going to Chelsea.'
'But me and the wife have booked to go to Charlton, and we want to go to Charlton.'
'Look, will you listen? The match is off at Charlton.'
'We are not going to no bloody match, we are going to the wife's sisters in Charlton to see her. We are not interested in any football match, we saw this cheap trip advertised to Charlton.'
'Go and sit down, I am trying to drive here, we will try and sort something out when we get there.'

On the outskirts of the capital, the driver pulled into a kerb, and calling the passenger who was so keen to see his sister-in-law to the front, arranged to drop him and his wife at Victoria coach station, with the proviso that he would pick up the pair at six o'clock and 'don't be late'. After doing what seemed like a tour of every street in London, I remember we managed to park at something called 'Parsons Green', and like a flock of provincial sheep on a day out, we eventually found Stamford Bridge. All I remember is Chelsea won 6-2 in a thoroughly entertaining game. We stopped at a M1 service station on the way back, and I spotted the original Finglands coach I should have travelled on. I quickly worked out that if I travelled to Ashton on Mayne's coach and arrived back at ten o'clock, the man in the Jag was unlikely to be waiting to give me a lift back to Didsbury, and if I wanted to be dropped off near home, I needed to get myself on the Finglands coach, their garage being not to far from where I lived. After a chat with both drivers, it was agreed that I could transfer onto my original choice of transport, which I duly did. I detected a glum and somewhat mutinous air amongst my fellow travellers, and asked how went their day.

'Go to another match?'
'The coach driver would not hear of it. "More than my job's worth. Charlton's where we are suppose to go and Charlton's where we are going.'

He would not even let them go to another game on public transport, while he waited at The Valley. He left at the precise time he should have left, had the match been played.

Kit Symons leads the players out for a friendly against Tianjin, before flash flooding hit China and caused the rest of the tour to be cancelled.

The only football the City fans on that coach got that afternoon was a kick about on a saturated coach park. By the way, if you should stumble across two mummified corpses in Victoria coach station, you will know how they got there and where they came from. You see, the driver of the Mayne's coach never went within five miles of that venue after we had left Parsons Green. Probably more than his job was worth.

John Maddocks
(This article first appeared in the City fanzine King of the Kippax *and was used with the permission of Joyce, the widow of John, who sadly passed away in March 2001.)*

And I Love You So

Watching Manchester City – well I was once in a party of ten or so people who embarked on a 12,000 mile round trip to watch one game of football. When we flew out to the Far East, we had expected to see three games, before flash flooding reduced the tour to one game. The trip started well when we spotted a few blokes in City tracksuits browsing in the duty-free at Heathrow airport. Gerry Creaney came over and started talking to us: he was amazed, and could not really believe we were travelling to China to watch City. In-flight entertainment was provided by the whole City squad with their medley of hits from the 1960s and '70s. The first of the three games was to be played in Tianjin, and when we got there we were told that the tour had been called off because of a national state of emergency, due to China's worst flooding for 150 years, and only the game in Tianjin would take place. As nobody knew the way to the ground, we followed the team coach in our minibus and found ourselves driving through the gates of the ground. The Tianjin fans must have wondered what sort of team they were facing when we piled out of the bus, unaware that the actual team were still sitting on the coach in front of us. Alan Ball gave a trial to Australian striker Damien Mori, and the team were one down after eighteen minutes. Mass changes for the second half saw Creaney make it one apiece. The score remained at 1-1, setting up a penalty shoot-out which seemed to go on for ages and ages, and when Lee Crooks was made to take his three times, it was obvious that we were not going to win the game. The Tianjin players reacted as though they had won the World Cup. In the evening, several of the team were relaxing in the hotel bar and had a go on the karaoke, and Alan Ball impressed with his version of 'And I love you so' by Perry Como. The following morning we had to change our flights, to make sure we were back in England in time for a friendly match at Scarborough.

Wilson Pratt

Not The Florida Special

The usual rumours started up regarding end-of-season and pre-season tours for the Blues. At the time, details were always difficult to get hold of, as fans were not being encouraged to follow City abroad because of hooliganism. Then, in April, the big one broke – the Alan Hudson Transatlantic Soccer Classic 1991 in Florida. For most, including us, it was a pipe dream. Adverts for a package deal appeared in a couple of City home programmes, and after a lot of soul-searching and the Barclaycard being scrutinized, we were in. We must have been mad, but what the hell. The whole thing gathered momentum. The tournament included City, Celtic, Sheffield Wednesday and Nottingham Forest. We knew there was a slight doubt about the official sanction, but there was no turning back, as you had to book early. Then the whole world fell in. I got a phone call from Colin Lund: 'its off', he said, 'But they are trying to change it to Bermuda'. The following week, Eddie Phillips in the souvenir shop was giving people their deposits back for the official trip. There was no real reason why the trip had been cancelled. Anyway, for whatever reason it was off, and it left hundreds of fans shocked, puzzled, angry, disappointed and broke.

Dave Wallace

Long And Winding Road

In a long hitchhiking career, there are not many places I have not been to, so when City announced they were planning a summer tour to Italy, I hit the long and winding road. The following is my diary of events.

Monday 27 July

Thumbed it down to Dover before zipping across the Channel on a jet foil to meet a mate of mine. After plundering a few local bars, we pitched our tent in a nearby park. A great idea this, even if the local constabulary didn't quite see it the same way, giving us half

FOLLOW CITY TO FLORIDA for the TRANSATLANTIC SOCCER CLASSIC

During the Summer, City are to play in a pre-season tournament in Florida, U.S.A., competing against Celtic, Nottingham Forest and Sheffield Wednesday.

Worlds End Travel have organised a special 15 day holiday, with tickets guaranteed for ALL matches in the tournament, with hotel accommodation in Tampa (8 nights) and Orlando (6 nights).

Depart from Manchester Airport—Friday 19th July. Return to Manchester Airport—Saturday 3rd August. £799 per person (child up to 16 years, sharing room with 2 adults—£499).

Price includes: Return flights Manchester/Orlando, Hotel accommodation, car hire (14 days), match tickets, airport taxes.

Special discount vouchers are also available for many Florida attractions.

A full itinerary and booking application forms can be obtained from the City Souvenir Shop (tel: 061-226-4824).

An advert placed in City's match magazine for the ill-fated trip to Florida.

an hour to move, or have the tent confiscated. We moved around the corner and weren't troubled again.

Tuesday 28 July

We made swift and steady progress past Brussels, through Luxembourg and on down to the outskirts of Metz in France where we waited ... and waited ... and waited ... for about five hours. Thinking we were heading for Strasbourg, little did we realise that we were facing in completely the opposite direction. That night we shared a service station with half-a-dozen wagons, two caravans and a plague of rats. Good old France!

Wednesday 29 July

After much more of the same on the following day, we took the bus right into Metz and, after a few (or perhaps several) scoops, we again attempted to reach Strasbourg, but France's reputation as a hitcher-hiker's graveyard totally put paid to that idea – so much so that at one point, I was prepared to call it a day and go all the way home. The night was spent in propping up a local hotel bar and then under canvas on a local camping site. Now we had been set back by almost a day-and-a-half, the following evening's game in Brescia looked even more distant than ever before.

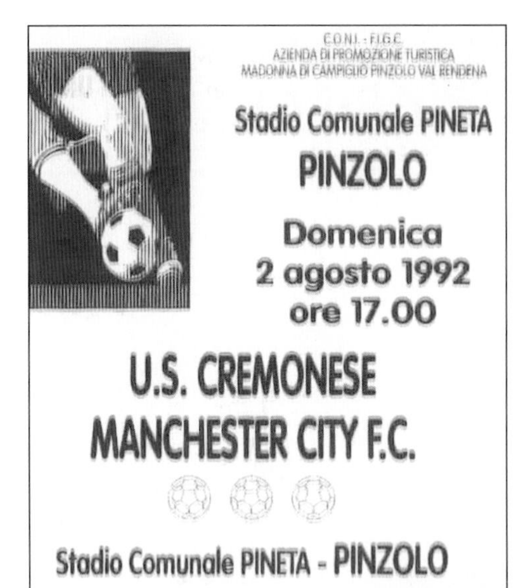

A poster advertising one of City's pre-season games in Italy against Cremonese.

Thursday 30 July

Having exhausted all five auto-stop (hitch-hiking) spots, we were forced to resort to taking the train to Strasbourg, and so two hours and 100 French francs later, we arrived there. Here again, the autostrada was a dead loss, and so, eventually, we walked across the Rhine Bridge at the Place de l'Europe and into Germany. Before long, a couple of lifts took us through Offenburg and down the autobahn to a Rasthaus near Freiburg. Unfortunately though, the fiver that I'd changed at the border was nowhere sufficient here! We'd missed the first game by now, so we looked towards the next game on the Sunday in Pinzolo. A mere two lifts later, and we were dropped off at the Swiss frontier near Basle. After a wait of several hours, another two lifts took us to Lucerne followed by a good lift into the Swiss Alps. A traffic jam together with bad weather dissuaded our driver from taking us through the St Gotthard Pass, and instead we were dropped off at the small village of Goshenen, where torrential rain kept us holed up in one of the town's two hotels/bars, although the local station afforded us the comparative luxury of a dilapidated railway carriage to spend the night in.

Saturday 31 July

Despite the Milano road signs in site, optimism of the new dawn was quietly strangled to death, and even the panoramic backdrop of mountains couldn't really compensate for the torturous five-and-a half-hour wait. We gave up at around dinner-time, eventually taking the train through the mountains to Bellinzona. After a quick change of money, an even quicker scoop, we took the bus to the nearest motorway junction. Amazingly, we got a lift after about an hour to the outskirts of Lugano, which is just about the last town before Italy. Confident that we would be in Milan later that night, our patience was eventually eroded, as hour after hour slipped by. So near, yet so far! We eventually traipsed down to the local village of Paradiso. Over yet another quick scoop, we learned that today was the National Swiss holiday: no wonder we could not get a lift! So without further ado, we took the train to Lugano and joined in the celebrations, and here we had a lucky break when we discovered that the trip to Milano's Bertrand station only cost a fiver.

Sunday 1 August

The train was late, almost an hour late. It was gone two in the morning when it turned up and four in the morning when it rolled into

Milan. There were people asleep everywhere, in the waiting room, on every bench and we quickly joined them. We rose early, at 7 a.m. and hung about for the train to Verona. Time was short, as the game was that afternoon, and we had only just found out where Pinzolo was. We got off at Verona and waited for the 2 p.m. train to Trento from where we had to take a bus to reach Pinzolo. Investigations revealed that the next bus to Pinzolo went at five o'clock and took one-and-a-half hours to get there. Left with no option, we thumbed a lift in a matter of minutes to within ten miles of our intended destination. Another lift saw us reach Pinzolo with five minutes to spare before the kick-off, or so we thought. The match against Italian side Cremonese had only kicked off half-an-hour early. The setting was idyllic – the pitch surrounded by pine trees and mountains beyond – it was little more than a park that had been fenced off, yet they still wanted a fiver for admission. Some of us sauntered through a gate and with the City players on the field and all the City fans grouped in a corner; it was truly an amazing sight. It was 1-1 (White) by this time, although the newly-returned Paul Lake put City 2-1 up, only for the Italians to equalize from about fifty miles offside, and there the score remained. After the 2-2 draw with Cremonese, everybody piled into the nearby bar and all the regular City fans were there. We did not get to see any other games on the tour, mainly due to poor organization: shame really, because we had to hitch all the way back to Manchester. But that's another story.

Noel Bayley

I remember going to watch a City home game some time in the 1980s, only to find it was called off, so Tina and I went to Port Vale, and Colin and a couple of others went to Wigan! I've since done Wigan, but he's not

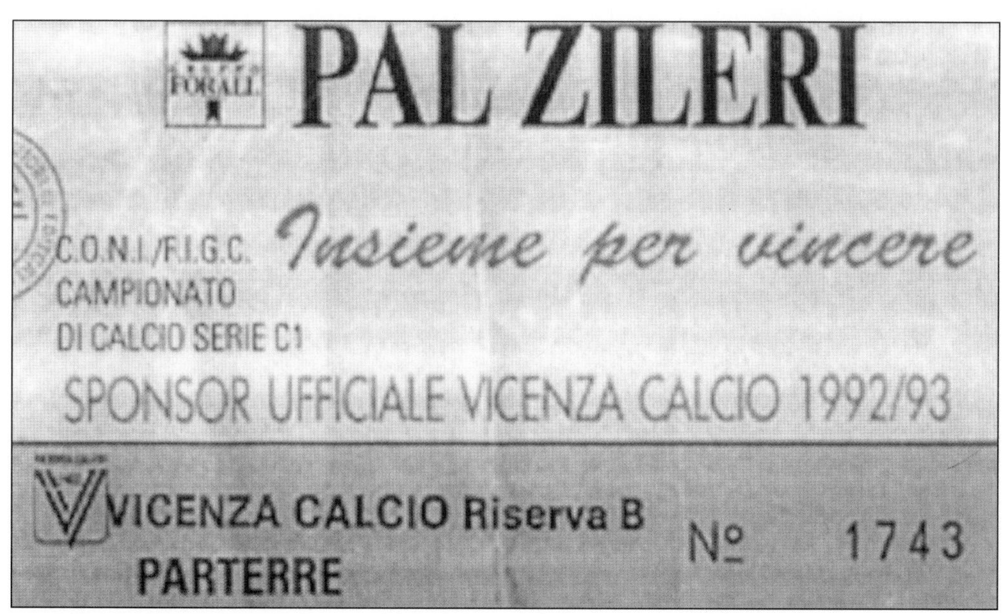
PAL ZILERI

C.O.N.I./F.I.G.C.
CAMPIONATO
DI CALCIO SERIE C1

Insieme per vincere

SPONSOR UFFICIALE VICENZA CALCIO 1992/93

VICENZA CALCIO Riserva B
PARTERRE
№ 1743

A ticket from the game played against Cremonese.

Early birds arrive at Wembley Way, ready to welcome their team to the play-off final.

done PV yet! Also, the time we were travelling to Derby and we had a spare reserved seat on the train (I was the London Branch travel organizer at the time, so they were in my name), a bloke sits down next to me, we got chatting then he asked what sort of group we were. I smiled sweetly at him and said football supporters – you've never seen anyone move so fast in your life! He left to our laughter ringing in his ears.

Carol Darvill

When Manchester United played Bayern Munich in the European Cup Final in Barcelona in May 1999, City were approaching the Second Division play-off final with Gillingham. We watched the Reds' game in McCormack's pub on Third Avenue in New York, the place packed with United fans, the Irish bartenders and even the Newcastle and Arsenal and Liverpool expatriates noisily supporting them too. While they celebrated United's victory, we resolved to go to see City, so at noon on Sunday 30 May we were wandering Wembley's streets looking for tickets. Jennifer had liberated a large Metropolitan Police sign from a lamp-post, the back of it handily turned into a 'Tickets Wanted' notice, and outside a pub a bloke offered two in the Gillingham end. Warned by the stewards to say nothing, we sat through the match in silence in the cold and the damp, and at 2-0 down got up and left. 'But they might do what United did', Jennifer protested, with typical American optimism – well, of course, I knew there was no chance of that. On Wembley Way, City fans streaming out of the stadium were suddenly cavorting around, somehow it had gone from 0-2 to 2-2, and we ran from pub to pub, in search of one that wasn't locked. At "Eddie's", we saw extra time and penalties – a comeback even more remarkable than United's, because this was City and City didn't do that. A year on, and City were at Blackburn, 7 May 2000, hoping for another promotion. Sunday morning landed at Manchester airport, on up to Blackburn, and this time didn't even get a sniff of a ticket, watched the game in a pub. It was very quiet at 1-0 down and the news coming through that Ipswich were winning. The cameras held a shot of a young lad in a City shirt inside the ground, his hands over his face in despair. Then someone stole the television. All eyes had been fastened on the set as Horlock's cross came over, but when Goater hoofed the ball into the goal there were bodies and beer everywhere, and by the time we could stand upright again the TV was off its brackets and was disappearing out the door. We heard, rather than saw, the rest of the game, standing outside Ewood listening to the roars of the crowd and to what the Rovers fans said as they poured out. Whatever he does in the future, Mark Kennedy will always be remembered for slotting home the third goal, then putting on that goofy grin and running half the length of the pitch into Joe Royle's arms. Someone later said he looked so smart in that red and black strip he could have gone straight to a wedding. If so, Dickov's goal to make it four was the icing on the cake, and City were up. We went back to Manchester and sat outside the Old Wellington in Shambles Square with a couple of Holland's meat pies. When we got back to Ringway next morning we'd spent just 27 hours in Lancashire. There must have been others who made the trip, for as we went through to the plane there was a celebratory song coming from behind: 'Who the f*** are Man United?', much to the amusement of the armed policemen standing by passport control.

Ken Corfield and Jennifer Wallace

Five of us travelled to watch City's two-game tour of Scotland in August 1984. This took in games at Hibernian on a Friday evening and Partick Thistle on a Sunday. Staying in Edinburgh on the Friday, we travelled over to Ayr on the west coast for the Saturday evening, not wishing to be in Glasgow for too long. This being in the days before TV decided kick-off times, if a game wasn't played on a Saturday afternoon, it was played in the evening, so we all assumed that it would be an evening kick-off. So as we entered Glasgow, we paid a short visit to Ibrox in the afternoon, before looking for Firhill. After numerous locals giving us directions, we found the stadium, and as we drove down a steep hill towards the ground, we could see a game was in progress – pre-match entertainment, we assumed, until it suddenly

Programme from the game against Hibernian.

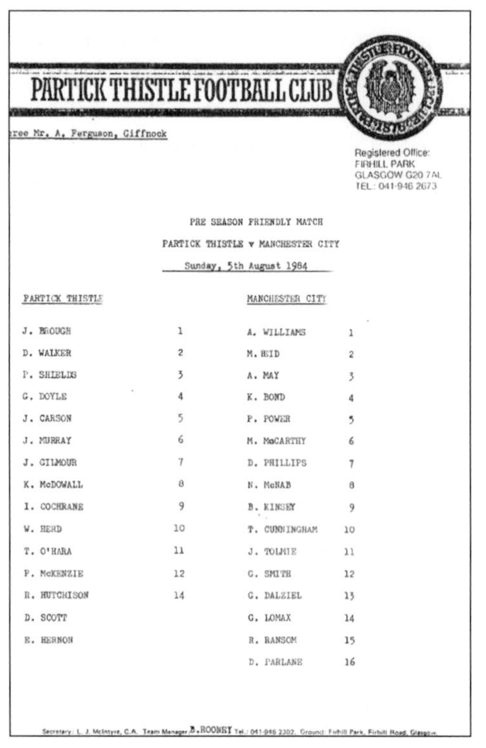

PARTICK THISTLE FOOTBALL CLUB

ree Mr. A. Ferguson, Giffnock

Registered Office:
FIRHILL PARK
GLASGOW G20 7AL
TEL: 041-946 2673

PRE SEASON FRIENDLY MATCH

PARTICK THISTLE v MANCHESTER CITY

Sunday, 5th August 1984

PARTICK THISTLE		MANCHESTER CITY	
J. BROUGH	1	A. WILLIAMS	1
D. WALKER	2	M. REID	2
P. SHIELDS	3	A. MAY	3
G. DOYLE	4	K. BOND	4
J. CARSON	5	P. POWER	5
J. MURRAY	6	M. McCARTHY	6
J. GILMOUR	7	D. PHILLIPS	7
K. McDOWALL	8	N. McNAB	8
I. COCHRANE	9	B. KINSEY	9
W. HERD	10	T. CUNNINGHAM	10
T. O'HARA	11	J. TOLMIE	11
P. McKENZIE	12	G. SMITH	12
R. HUTCHISON	14	G. DALZIEL	13
D. SCOTT		G. LOMAX	14
E. HERNON		R. RANSOM	15
		D. PARLANE	16

Secretary: L. J. McIntyre, C.A. Team Manager B. ROONEY Tel.: 041-946 2302. Ground: Firhill Park, Firhill Road, Glasgow.

Programme from the game against Partick Thistle.

dawned on us that City were playing and it was an afternoon kick-off! We parked up outside, got in for free as the exit gates were open, to find City were losing 3-0 with only five minutes left. At least we managed to see City's consolation goal.

Phill Gatenby

Considering the number of seasons (forty-six) I've been following City away, I've been pretty lucky with avoiding disastrous trips, although bringing up a family on one wage (aw!) far from any help from relatives, did curtail European adventures. London trips in the 1950s, when I was a lad, were always long and drawn-out affairs. I used to bike it from Swinton to London Road (now Piccadilly) station; catch the 12.30 a.m. train, arriving in the capital in the early hours. Spotting the tramps, playing football in Hyde Park, traipsing around the sights, we'd finally arrive at the relevant ground around one-ish, in time for the 3.00 p.m. kick-off. Then, after the game, maybe there would be chance for a chat with the players if they were on our train back to Manchester. (Bert Trautmann once read my notebook and suggested that I was a budding journalist. Sorry, Bert, I should've worked harder at school!) Then biking it back from the station, I'd arrive home around midnight. Usually after a loss! I remember once – 1959, I think – the Supporters' Club played West Ham Supporters' Club in the morning, in the fog, losing about 11-1. The fog cleared, and the result was announced at the game, to great guffaws, as we went on to lose 4-1! Then there was the abandoned game at Luton in 1961. 2-0 down after a quarter-of-an-hour, 3-2 up at half-time, when the ref (Tuck of Chesterfield) could, and should, have abandoned it. The score was 6-2 with twenty minutes to go, all our goals scored by Dennis. Total frustration and anger when it was finally abandoned, and, of course, we lost the replay, 3-1! I was locked out at Leeds in '68, when we lost 2-0. The train for the League Cup tie in '89 arrived at Brentford at half-time. We lost 2-1, and it didn't augur well for the following Saturday's game *v.* the Rags (won 5-1?). In 1993, we survived the inevitable car crash on the way to Coventry to see us go 2-0 down and win 3-2; and we arrived at Spurs in torrential rain in '95 to find that although the rain stopped and things brightened, the game was, nevertheless, called off – much to John Burridge's disgust! The oft-postponed midweek cup tie against Brentford in '97 meant taking the afternoon off work, and we arrived in plenty of time only to find that the game was off due to frost. We had a new issue due out on the following Saturday, so the 200 copies of the current issue, carefully saved for this cup game, had to go to the tip. Probably the most traumatic 'away' game, however, was after the 1-0 home defeat on a foggy November Manc day in '69 (23,861, incidentally, at Maine Road). A late night return to our then home in Sheffield, with a blown head gasket on top of the Snake Pass, which gave us nightmares as we rolled the car down to the Snake Inn, where we were refused a bed for the night. After calling out the AA, we were towed back to Glossop, where Sue and I spent the night at Glossop police station – on the games room benches, not in a cell!

Dave Wallace

Gaytours

After watching United win the Euro Cup in May 1968, my late father promised if City ever get to a Euro final, he would pay for me to go. I can't remember what date, but I remember ringing one Saturday night – from about 4.30 to exactly 6 p.m. – a travel firm in Deansgate called, unfortunately, 'Gaytours'. They were the only firm offering flight and seat tickets, we had all but given up, when at 10 seconds to six o'clock (six being their closing time), they answered and I, at fifteen, who had never been on a plane before, let alone abroad, was on my way. The big problem now was school and my CSE examinations: I had one on the 28, and two on the 30. But none on the 29. Morning of the 29, up at 4 a.m., Mother scared to death, me on an absolute high. Flew at 6.30 a.m., arrived at 8.30 a.m. and went on the sight-seeing tour arranged with the ticket. Got to the ground about 5.30 p.m., saw the lads arrive, and then went into the ground. Fabulous stadium, only problem was it had no roof, and it only had about 8,000 in it – only about 300 were allowed out of Poland, but it held about 80,000. Then this programme seller tried to take money off me, but a big guy dressed in blue said it had 'gratis' written on the front. The game kicked off and then the rain came – anyone who was there would tell you, it never rains like that in Manchester – some took shelter in the tunnels, but most (including me) stood out in it. The final whistle went, and a 2-1 win was just the most incredible feeling I ever had, or probably will ever experience. It made everything that was hard about being a Blue seem worthwhile, and all the pain since can usually be brushed aside eventually by casting my memory back to that night, and the memory that no one can ever take off me. The trip back to the airport and the flight back was memorable for the amount of water running off people, and running down the coach/plane, and the incredible storm when we took off from Vienna Airport – almost everyone by this time was using their small paper bag. Arrived home at about 5.30 a.m., had an hour's sleep, then went off to school for my nine o'clock exam in English – an essay –and by 10.30 a.m., it was being written on two or three lines.

Mike Ash

CHAPTER 6
Why Blue?

Even a sudden downpour could not dampen these City supporters at the Wembley play-off final.

Why do you support City?

Fat John

This may seem a strange thing to say, but I've found that my fortunes in life are often reflected in City's performances on the pitch. Of course, this isn't entirely true, if it was I'd have been really miserable for the past twenty-two years. But it works to an extent. For example, two seasons ago, I had a good job, was blissfully happy with my girlfriend and City gained promotion to the Premier League, following a dramatic final-day-of-the-season 4-1 victory over Blackburn Rovers. By December, I had lost my job and City responded by losing six games on the trot. The team slid relentlessly towards relegation and my girlfriend moaned and moaned about my inability to find work. She eventually walked out, just twelve hours before a brave City side were beaten 2-1 at Portman Road and relegated to Division One. This kind of thing has been going on for years; the loss of my one true love coincided with the relegation of Joe Royle's side to Division Two back in 1998. There was no silver lining to the cloud that was losing my girlfriend Claire, but there was in going down to Division Two. For if we hadn't have gone down, and if we hadn't have played so badly at the beginning of the season, we would never have gone to Wembley in the play-offs, and I would never have experienced the happiest, most wonderful moment of my life. I watched the play-off final against Gillingham in York. I was unable to attend the match as my dissertation was due in just two days later, so I settled for watching the game in a pub with the only other three Blues I knew in the whole university: Fat John, Salford Tom and Nick. At kick-off, I was desperately trying not to be sick. I had never been this nervous in my life. Eighty-three agonizing minutes later, Bob Taylor scored the only decent goal he'd ever score in a game involving Manchester City, and we looked dead and buried. We were 2-0 down, and my soul sank to a new depth. We were finished. It was the most important match of my life and we had lost it to Gillingham. City had hurt me so many times before, but there had never been anything like this. This had gone too far. This wasn't funny. For the first time in my life, I questioned what I was doing and fleetingly considered whether this was all worthwhile. I was gripped with denial; we were going to be promoted. We had to be, I had been so sure. Fat John who, with tears streaming down his face, showed his sportsmanship by throwing an ashtray fifteen metres across the pub, broke my concentration. It smashed above the heads of the gleeful Gillingham fans. It was a horrible moment. Out of nowhere, the ex-'one true love' Claire appeared and presented me with a pint of lager. She said I looked like I needed it. They were the first words either of us had spoken to the other in six months. Though I'd been teetotal all week whilst I'd been desperately finishing my dissertation, I figured that she was right. If I ever needed or deserved a drink, it was now. On my birthday in June of the previous year, Claire had taken me down to the banks of the River Ouse and treated me to a midnight picnic. She produced a small Jamaica cake (my favourite delicacy) bearing a single candle. She lit it and told me I could make a wish when I blew it out. She guaranteed it would come true. I looked at her and realised she was the most perfect girl I would ever meet. She was beautiful, an angel, and I was truly happy. My mind raced as to what I should wish for, should I wish to marry this girl or wish that we'd be happy together for the rest of our lives. Then the instincts of twenty torturous years intervened, and I wished that Manchester City would gain promotion back to the Nationwide Division One at the first attempt. About two months after my birthday, I'd just made Claire lunch when she asked me if I had made any plans for our future together. I replied, with some pride, that I'd purchased tickets for us both for City's first game of the season at home to Blackpool. She looked taken aback and replied that she'd meant living together in London or maybe even getting engaged after university. 'They're good seats', I mumbled quietly. A few weeks later, she left me for an old boyfriend from down south, and I can't say I ever blamed her. If only I could have made her see how perfect she was, or if only I'd been articulate enough to express how I felt about her. If only I hadn't bought her a Manchester City away shirt. And so, here she stood on play-off final day, eleven months later, offering me a drink. I remembered my birthday wish: I didn't want her Stella Artois; she owed me a result. With mere seconds left in the game and City 2-0 down, the ball broke to Shaun Goater on the edge of the

Paul Dickov scores the goal that made him a modern-day hero amongst the City faithful.

Gillingham area. He was clean through on goal. Thankfully, before the Goat could unleash one of his clinical finishes, he was tackled and the ball broke to Kevin Horlock, who swept it into the unguarded net. I stood up and screamed; though none of the others did. A group of girls eating their Sunday lunch laughed at me. I didn't care. There was no way they could have understood. They say the Lord moves in mysterious ways. If there is a God, then this was the moment when he or she decided that enough was enough. The referee inexplicably found five minutes of stoppage time and, despite Gareth Taylor's attempts to run down the clock by arguing with him for a good minute-and-a-half, City surged forward. In the dying seconds of the ninety-fifth minute, a hopeful ball into the Gillingham half of the field found Goater on the edge of the penalty area, he bundled the ball in the direction of Paul Dickov. Despite being marked by three Gillingham defenders, Dicky managed to spin on the ball and unleash a shot. I have been suffering at the hands of Manchester City all my life. I can still clearly remember crying when Luton Town relegated us on the final day of the 1982/83 season. I was four years old. Four more relegations have followed since then; there have been eighteen years of false dawns and false promises. Eighteen years of Peter Swales and Francis Lee. Of Alan Ball, Steve Coppell and Frank Clark. Eighteen years of Old Trafford defeats, Kanchelskis hat-tricks and Eric Cantona. Of watching Steve Lomas keeping the ball by the corner flag when we actually needed to score. Eighteen years of ten goals at Anfield in four days. Of playing Macclesfield in front of a few thousand in your local derby. Eighteen years of Tony

Vaughan, Gareth Taylor and Lee Bradbury. I suffered at the hands of Manchester City, I gave them my heart and, to be frank, I got very little back in return. But I never stopped believing in them, and I never gave up hope. Perhaps if I had, and perhaps if I hadn't suffered as much as I did, what happened on 30 May 1999 would not have been as glorious as it was. Dickov's shot found the top corner of the Gillingham net. It was the most extraordinary, exhilarating moment of my life and it made every painful moment of the previous eighteen years worthwhile. It's funny, but the thing I remember the most about the goal was that my friend Martyn (who wasn't really a football fan) was screaming too. He said afterwards that he had suddenly felt like he was nine years old. The occasion had got to all of us. Dicky skidded onto his knees on the sodden Wembley turf, and a few hundred miles away in a pub in York, I mirrored his actions. I turned to the others and noticed that Fat John, Salford Tom and Nick were all crying. It was a wonderful moment, one that I'll always remember. About forty minutes later, Nicky Weaver saved Guy Butter's penalty and Manchester City were promoted to Division One. Weaver famously sprinted off down the Wembley turf, dodging one City player after another, until Andy Morrison dragged him to the ground. I didn't see any of this. The table we'd been watching the game around had collapsed under Fat John's celebrations and we were all on the floor. Though none of us really knew each other that well, we embraced as if we had been friends our whole lives. It was perfect. I hugged a confused looking Claire and thanked her. She had not let me down after all. She'd kept her promise and my faith in life was restored. Given that my wish came true, one might argue that I sacrificed a lifetime of happiness with the girl of my dreams in return for one good result. It's a decision I've never questioned. There's a great misconception that it must be hard being a Manchester City supporter. That perhaps we're all a bit strange or glutton for further punishment. The truth is, that watching Manchester City is compelling, enthralling and completely addictive, since the end of every season provokes such powerful emotions; be it the euphoria of promotion or the heartache of relegation. City may occasionally do the most farcical things, but I'd rather turn up to watch a match knowing that something extraordinary will happen, even if it's bad. The characters may change every now and again, but the soap opera that is Manchester City lives on. The fact that it's all so dramatic and nonsensical makes it all the more watchable. If it was scripted, people would complain that it was too ridiculous, and I'd rather have that than be mid-table Premier League for the rest of my life. So what about relegation, unemploy-

Nicky Weaver saves Gillingham's fourth penalty and secures promotion for City.

Malcom Allison – City fans will always remember the days when he worked with Joe Mercer to bring the great days back to Maine Road.

ment and girlfriends who don't understand? There's always next season. My luck's bound to change then.

Matthew Roberts

New To Earth

I was born and bred in Sunderland, but have lived in East Yorkshire for most of the last eighteen years, apart from the three years I spent at Leeds University. I could never remember exactly when I got interested in City, but have a vague recollection of it being in my primary school days. With hindsight, I reckon it coincided with the purple patch at the end of the 1960s and early '70s, when City actually won things, so I suppose I was something of a bandwagon jumper at the time, though you can forgive an eight-year-old that much! However, I guess I forgot to jump off the bandwagon thereafter, and though I tell myself football's not that important, I still can't help feeling happy or down in the dumps depending on how the results go. As one of the famous Gallaghers said (sort of), you'd never tell an alien new to Earth to support City, as it would be too much like hard work! Being a City supporter as a teenager in the North East wasn't an easy option. Almost all my mates were Sunderland supporters, and whilst they didn't have much to crow about, they could at least get to Roker Park easily. I have a confession to make – I've only ever made it to Maine Road once in all these years, but have been to away games wherever the opportunity has arisen – Newcastle, Sunderland, Hull, Leeds. That one occasion was, predictably, for a game against Sunderland (went with my Dad) – the FA Cup fifth round game in 1973! My life was hell for weeks after the replay, and I cursed Allison for winding up the Sunderland team beforehand.

Geoff Donkin

So Many Memories

My boyhood friend Kenny Moss supported City, so I became a City fan too. I think Kenny used to go to matches, which I really admired him for. Those were the days when Dave Ewing was scoring an own goal every week. Anyway, during the early part of the 1962/63 season, I eventually went to Maine Road as an eleven-year-old and witnessed City get thrashed 6-1 by West Ham. Bert Trautmann was sent off, and it was on the national news when I got back home to

Langley at 6.00 p.m. I have got so many memories of Manchester City. Here are a few in the order that I think of them. The last day of the Kippax Stand was fantastic, and it elevated my interest in City to a new level. Seeing the old players come onto the pitch choked me up, especially Mike Summerbee, who I loved in his playing days at Maine Road. I couldn't stop myself crying for about fifteen minutes, and me a tough Langley lad! My first really emotional moment at Maine Road was seeing my other favourite, Johnny Crossan, holding that Second Division Trophy aloft in 1966. He may not have been a Gio Kinkladze, but he was to me during my school days. I was always inside right at school, pretending to be either Crossan, Colin Bell or Bally. I know most City fans probably regret the appointment of Alan Ball to the City manager's job, but to me it was a dream come true. My favourite players when I was a kid were Colin Bell, Mike Summerbee, Alan Ball and Johnny Crossan. I became friendly with Bally before he joined City, because he was a frequent visitor to Jersey, and he invited me to his office before the first game of one season against Spurs. That was really an exciting moment for me. Colin Bell's comeback against Newcastle was unbelievable. The applause must have gone on for about fifteen minutes. The tears of happiness that were shed during that time because their hero Colin Bell was back playing again must be one of the greatest moments in Man City's history. He was the best player ever to me. The 3-1 win at Old Trafford in 1968 was fantastic. We knew we were a good team, but that result proved to everybody that we could be the best. Colin Bell's shot would have hit me, if the United net had not got in the way. You never forget these moments. The Tommy Booth goal at Villa Park in 1969 was another fabulous moment for City fans. I didn't make the cup final because London was a long way for an eighteen-year-old in those days. I watched the match at my home with about five pals and plenty of booze, and the good win set us up for the evening. Newcastle in 1968 had everything. Goals going in at both ends. We didn't know which way it would go, but the news filtered through that United had lost and that made us Champions. We ran on the pitch, and nobody seemed to mind too much. Joe Mercer was on the radio saying what a great team we were. I got back to Manchester at about 11.00 p.m. and was in the Twisted Wheel by 12.00 p.m. That will mean something to older Mancunians. Crazy, wonderful

City fans were unimpressed with the appointment of Alan Ball, wanting a highly-successful profile manager with a proven track-record, as they had been promised.

day. Spurs in 1981 FA Cup Final. I thought we were the better team in the first match. We stayed over in London for the replay, and a Tottenham fan broke my nose before the game. I was trying to get my mate's flag off him that he had pinched. It was like Custer's last stand. I had to charge the guy, so at least he missed the match. A policeman was nearby and had witnessed the whole thing, and persuaded me to go down to Wembley station with him. I thought Steve McKenzie's goal was better than Villa's. I used to go to the matches in the 1960s with Les Saul and his nephew. We would stand in the Kippax, same spot every game. Noodle soup at half-time. Mostly good results at home in those days. I liked Derek Kevan, Jimmy Murray and Matt Gray in my earliest days. Another great player was Dennis Tueart; he should have won 60 England caps. Whenever he had the ball, he would go for goal. He scored a lot for a winger. Thanks to him, we won the League Cup – that was another smashing side we had back then. Denis Law's back-heel. That was special. Those were great days. I remember we had great fun getting off the special buses in Piccadilly in an effort to get about twenty *Pink* newspapers for the lads on the bus. We would jump off the bus and would hope we could catch the same bus before it left the next stop. We had about forty-five seconds to persuade the paper-seller to give us twenty Pinks very, very quickly, otherwise we were landed with them and the bus was gone. These were the old type of bus, remember. We could have easily been killed, but we were young, and if City had won we wanted to read about it. I felt great sadness when I heard Joe Mercer had died. The book that was written about him was really good. He was a truly great, decent man. God bless him. The first home game at Maine Road in 1967 against the Champions, Liverpool. I thought we would get thrashed, having just been promoted, but a Colin Bell winner in the last few minutes sorted them out. What a thrill that was. I did love those night matches. The Blackburn 2 City 3 game a couple of years ago. What a fabulous performance that was. There was a great deal of sadness when it was reported that Mike Summerbee wanted a transfer in the mid-sixties. The third round FA Cup replay – City 3 Blackpool 1 (1966). Crossan, Summerbee, and Doyle scored, all great headers, especially Mike Doyle's goal. Alan Ball never got a kick, thanks to Dave Connor. There was a great atmosphere at the night matches in those days. The Kippax was really vocal. Smashing songs. 'Bladon Races', I think that was the proper name, was my

The official souvenir programme from the 100th FA Cup Final.

Left: *Dennis Tueart was one of the best forwards of his era. He was a fine striker, whose polished game excited crowds wherever he played.* Right: *Joe Mercer was one of the game's all-time greats, both as a player and as a manager. He was awarded an OBE for his services to football in 1976.*

favourite. It started 'His name was Colin Bell and he's the leader of our team, the greatest football team the world has ever seen'. Great night that. The despair in 1983 being relegated – I felt that the team had let down the club and all the great players that we had at Maine Road, since we were promoted in 1966. Leeds 1 City 0 (1967). This was a cup tie, I think. We completely dominated the game and Colin Bell missed three sitters. But this was also the game that proved to everybody that we could match the best, and we would only get better after this game, which we did. Beating Liverpool a couple of years ago with a Gaudino goal. All my family attended this match, and we met up with Mike Summerbee first. I had invited him to Jersey earlier in the year, and he entertained the City fans one evening. I really enjoyed that day with my two brothers and our wives, attending Maine Road for the first time. Since I left Manchester in 1979, I have been a big fan, but after that 1983 relegation, it seemed to go down my priority list a little. I suppose this was inevitable, after going to nearly every home match for seventeen years and my move to Jersey. The 1980s never really got going for me until Peter Reid arrived – two fifth spots put us back where we belonged. However, that Tottenham sixth round tie set us on the slide again, from which we have never recovered. I suppose the agony has gone on longer, but the great moments I have had were worth the pain. I only hope that the younger fans will see the same success one day.

Bob Young

My father was a Blue – he wouldn't eat bacon unless it was in a sandwich because it was red and white. My uncles and cousins were Blues. If you were called Talbot in Ashton-under-Lyne, you were Blue. It was as simple as that! My father took me, most Saturdays in the 1950s, to watch the Blues. I probably saw all but a handful of games at Maine Road, and a high proportion of away games between 1953 and the early 1970s. Nothing much changes with City – my first recollections were of relegation. We quickly bounced back that time, and put a squad together, which got us to Wembley in 1955. City, down to ten men after Jimmy Meadows was carried off in the nineteenth minute, eventually went down 3-1, to Jackie Milburn's Newcastle. They were back at Wembley within twelve months, this time beating Birmingham 3-1. Of course, those were the years of Don Revie, Bert Trautmann, Roy Paul, Bobby Johnson, Joe Hayes, and Nobby

Left: *Mike Summerbee was a star of the City side who won the First Division Championship in 1967/68. He was highly regarded as a fine ball-player, and won international honours with England.* Right: *Mike Doyle was one of the club's finest players during the Mercer/Allison reign. He was a determined performer in whatever role he was given.*

Clarke. My most emotional recollection of that period is not of Bert Trautmann holding his neck as he collected his winner's medal in 1956, but of Nobby Clarke being half carried, half dragged off the pitch, more like a black sack then a footballer, in the previous year's semi-final against Sunderland. Minutes earlier, in a mudbath of a pitch in pouring rain, Clarky had scored the only goal – Joe Hayes ran down the wing and hit it low into the penalty area. Clarky threw himself at it and headed into the bottom corner. His momentum slid him several yards through the mud. I can see now the look of pure joy on his face, as he wiped the mud from his eyes and peered at the ball in the net. By the mid-1950s, I was hooked. The late fifties was the Denis Law era. City busted the UK transfer record to buy him from Huddersfield, paying £55,000 (funny that it had the same impact then as Newcastle buying Shearer for £15 million a few years ago). Colin Barlow was also around at that time. The era ended when Denis went to Turin, City slid into the Second Division. Things became as bad in the mid-sixties as now. I was there on the Saturday when only 8,600 turned up at Maine Road. Somebody got the message. George Poyser went; Joe Mercer and Big Mal came. The rest is, as they say, history. The League win in 1968 was the thrill. Yes, I was in tears at St James Park as the final whistle went. (The only time I have cried at a City match – though, God knows, some performances were that bad, I should have cried.) Typical City, they kept us at the edge, eventually winning 4-3. The tannoy began to play Cliff Richard's hit 'Congratulations' within seconds of the final whistle. I cried for my dad, my uncles, my cousins and all the rest of our fans. The Newcastle fans were also singing, and I've had a soft spot for Newcastle ever since. The FA Cup, the League Cup, the

Maurizo Gaudino joined City on loan in December 1994 from Eintracht Frankfurt. He was an excellent footballer and, when in the mood, the opposition had to watch out. He currently plays his football in Turkey for Antalyaspo.

European Cup, and Cup-winners' Cup all followed. A few years ago, my father died. A few weeks earlier, my daughter rang City and told them about him (he was just a fan like the rest of us, no more, no less). I am not sure why she did it, I expected nothing. A couple of days later, an autographed City shirt arrived, together with a short letter from Brian Horton. This was at a time when his job was daily on the line. City is that type of club, with that type of fans.

Peter Talbot

The first holiday I can remember was in 1970 – a week in Torquay. My mother bought me

A programme from 'The Roy Clarke Evening', organized in tribute to a man who has been actively involved with City for longer than any other professional player.

a couple of t-shirts especially for the happy occasion: one red, which featured the Roadrunner, and the other sky-blue, featuring Bugs Bunny. On returning from the sunny South Coast, we visited my grandparents, and on our arrival there, my grandfather took one look at my red t-shirt and promptly exploded. 'Don't ever come here again wearing anything red!' he said. My grandfather may have been a lifelong Blue, and he may even have been amongst the 84,569 crowd that crowded into Maine Road for Stoke's visit in 1934, but black humour isn't something you readily understand at four years of age! Not to worry though, his advice stood me in good stead for the next twenty-seven years. Fast-forward to sometime later in my embryonic years, and a schoolyard in Wythenshawe provided the daily battleground for any number of games of City *v.* United. Difficult to imagine now, I know, but the numbers were fairly evenly matched back in the 1970s. Naturally, I took the City side, but if my grandfather's influence was subconscious, my father's was anything but. He hated City (called 'em the ragged eleven, and probably still does) and I hated him! He didn't care much for Led Zeppelin either, but then what did he know? It was a vicious circle. Our relationship deteriorated probably from the day I was born. He wouldn't take me to matches because he worked on Saturdays. That was his excuse, and just to make his point, I cannot recall him having a single Saturday off work in about five years. This only steeled my resolve. The day of reckoning came on 12 November 1975. City beat United 4-0 in a League Cup tie, and I was truly a believer (not that there was any doubt, of course). Now there was no going back. Of course I wasn't there, I was under my bedclothes, listening to the night's events unfold on a transistor radio the size of a house. Maine Road would have to wait almost another year to witness my debut. I doubt if anyone remembers the 0-0 draw with Newcastle on 6 November as, apart from Joe Corrigan chasing a black mongrel round the pitch, nothing much happened. For me, however, the memory of that day is vivid, even if the mighty Blues failed to score. My dad wasn't there, of course; my teacher Mr Murray took me, along with the rest of the school football team, on some free North Stand tickets. Oddly enough though, my father suffered a rare personality reversal some months later, when he had an ultra-rare Saturday off work and took me to a reserve game at Maine Road. Naturally, it wasn't the same as a first-team game, but while he was in an unusually good mood, he promised to take me to one and so, on 12 February 1977, I saw my first City goal from the Platt Lane Stand, as Joe Royle scored against Arsenal in a 1-0 win. My dad must have been well and truly upset, as he probably only went in the hope that City would lose! Still, he got his revenge a few years later by grounding me almost every time City were playing at home. It isn't much fun having to leave home almost every other weekend at fourteen, just so you can go to the match. In the end, he gave up on trying to stop me from going, and while he still can't get into Led Zep, there is no doubt that those early struggles probably explain why I have been prepared to move heaven and earth, lose out on sleep, girlfriends, holidays, and even work, in my quest to get to watch City at Maine Road.

Noel Bayley

Hailing from Gravesend in Kent (I now live in Bramhall, Cheshire), you would expect me to support someone like Arsenal, Spurs or even Gillingham! But no – despite the tried and tested efforts of my late father to get me to support Arsenal, I decided at the tender age of ten (in 1967) that City were for me. I thought Francis Lee and Colin Bell were the greatest (not a bad judge really, for a woman!), so my late granny said, 'If you're going to support two players, you'd better support the whole team'. There have been times since then when, much as I loved the old dear, I could have cheerfully strangled her! So, my allegiance grew steadily. My best mate Julie was, and still is, a raging Spurs fan, and even got me to wear a Spurs badge for ten minutes, but she got it back having failed to convert me. My first match was in the early 1970s when Spurs played City at White Hart Lane – Julie's dad took us. Even now, I

Newcastle – it's over, and what a thriller it was. City are crowned Champions, much to the delight of their supporters.

can't remember the actual date. I remember Alan Oakes was the sub that day and was warming up in front of us. Our places were near the City fans, as I remember seeing a girl from top to toe in blue and white. City won 3-2, and I was threatened with having to walk home if I said anything – they couldn't stop me grinning though! I joined the London Branch in 1976, just before the League Cup Final, and have been a member ever since. I met my husband, Colin, in 1979, before a Spurs away match, and we were married on 18 April 1981 (Wolves away – won 3-2!), the week after the FA Cup semi-final at Villa Park. In fact, I mentioned this to Paul Power at Bradford one season, and he said he had married three months after – and yes, we are both still with our respective spouses! We lived for eleven years about five minutes away from Leyton Orient's ground (great place!) and I often thought, as I waited for a bus to take me to Walthamstow Central to meet my mate Maggie, 'What the hell am I doing travelling 200-odd miles to see City, when I've got a football team on my doorstep?' Needless to say, until I moved 'up North' a few years ago, I kept thinking that thought but never did anything about it! The highlights of being a Blue – winning everything in sight when I first started supporting them; United getting relegated; 1976, of course, stuffing United 5-1; winning 10-1; getting promotion at Bradford in 1989; having the privilege of watching Gio Kinkladze and Trevor Francis in a blue shirt. I haven't mentioned Franny and Colin Bell, as they finished playing before I started to see City 'live'. Low points – continually getting beaten by United; having the fact that they are better than anyone on God's earth shoved down my throat whether I am 'back home' or up here; relegation three times; perpetual changes in management personnel; and the continual worry if we are going to hang on to our best players or not. Having said that, City are a team for life, they get under your skin, in your blood and, more often than not, right up your nose, but once a Blue, always a Blue – I couldn't see myself supporting anyone else ever. I suppose I'm like the song – I'm City till I die.

Carol Darvill

This may seem like a strange 'Why Blue?' because, unlike so many others, I never had to sneak off to Maine Road using a cover story, I wasn't in the record low crowd that day against Swindon, and I was never dragged off to Old Trafford by some well-meaning, but sadly misguided, red relative. I was born and raised in Gorton, my mother; my uncles (all three of them), my grandparents and my cousins were all Reds (though all but one uncle and his son were true Reds, i.e. never went near the ground, but had comfy armchairs). Fortunately, my father was a Blue, and had no intention of taking me anywhere near Trafford Park. I don't remember my first game in any detail, I can't remember who we played, but I remember sitting in the open bit between the Maine and North Stands (we always sat there, for some reason that escapes me). I think this was around 1975 (I would have been about seven) and what I do remember was that I loved it. The remainder of the 1970s is a bit of a blur: I remember attending matches, but none in any great detail; I idolized Peter Barnes and Dennis Tueart; admired big Dave Watson and Joe Corrigan; and wished I'd seen Colin Bell. I continued going until 1979, when after the Maine Road derby game (3-0 to them), I saw a young man stabbed in the leg. After this, my father stopped taking me, and I never asked to go again. The next eight years were a football wilderness for me; I showed little or no interest in football of any type and certainly didn't attend any games. I watched the 1981 FA Cup Final and replay and wanted City to win, but the passion had gone. I didn't relate my lack of interest in football to the stabbing incident and still don't, it was just one of those things; if it hadn't happened, I may have carried on going or may have just drifted away, another one of those 'What if?' questions that will never be answered. In 1987, I went to university in Liverpool, and while there, a friend persuaded me to go along and watch, of all teams, Tranmere Rovers. All I remember of the game was that they played Bristol Rovers, they lost and it was rubbish. Despite this, I found myself considering a trip to Maine Road, although I can't explain why; it was just an itch that needed to be scratched. On my next trip back to Manchester, I organized to take my father along to see a game – we stood on the Kippax, City won, and I was hooked all over again. That year, I travelled to as many games as my grant would allow, much to the bemusement of my parents, after years of living in Manchester and showing no interest. This continued until I finished university, got a job, and could afford a season ticket. Even though my new job was in Gloucester, I managed every home game and about half the away games for the next four seasons. In 1994, I briefly moved jobs to Warrington to be closer to home (closer to Maine Road, more like it), and then six months later accepted a job in Australia (*not* closer to Maine Road). Since then, I have been back once, taking in the first four games of the 1995/96 season (a draw and three losses, including trips to QPR and Coventry). I tune in the radio in the early hours every Sunday morning to get the results 'live', and spend hours scouring the net for every piece of information on the Blues I can obtain. There tend to be more downs than ups, we're unpredictable, frustrating and sometimes you just want to bang your head (or preferably a player's head) against a brick wall, but that's what it is to be a Blue! It's about humour, belonging and the pure, unadulterated, stubborn-minded knowledge that we are fighting the good fight. So 'Why Blue?' – well, I don't think it's something you choose, I think it's something that chooses you. Stay Blue.

Alan Oakes was a quiet unassuming player, who still holds the club record for most appearances – 668 games.

Gary King

Why Blue? That very question was put to me by a City fan I met recently [in America]. 'Are you from Manchester?' he asked, somewhat stunned to meet a fellow Blue supporter in this anti-footy nation, where, thanks to Sky TV, United are televised almost as often as the Dallas Cowboys. When I replied in the negative, with a clearly Yank twang, he shrugged and said: 'Well, I feel sorry for you then. I had no choice. My dad was a City man. I was born that way.' My excuse? Well, if I wanted to fabricate some justification, I could tell you that it was fate, being born in 1969, exactly one day after City's last FA Cup triumph. Or that I fell in love with Rodney Marsh when he played in our ill-fated North American Soccer League. Or that I live minutes from Manchester Avenue in the Los Angeles suburb of Inglewood, which is the truth, but not the reason I'm a true Blue, I must confess. It was the uniform. That's it. The beautiful Blue of City. Why Blue, indeed. The first time I saw it was in 1980, the days when the whole kit, from head to toe, was light blue. I was in Israel visiting family, as I did every other summer of my youth, and starving for sports. Back then, without CNN International, there was no way to follow baseball or other American pursuits in a country like Israel, which showed maybe two hours of local and European sport per week on its state-run channels. So, I begged my grandparents to find me something – anything – written in English for me to read. All they could locate was *Shoot*, which quickly became my bible. I

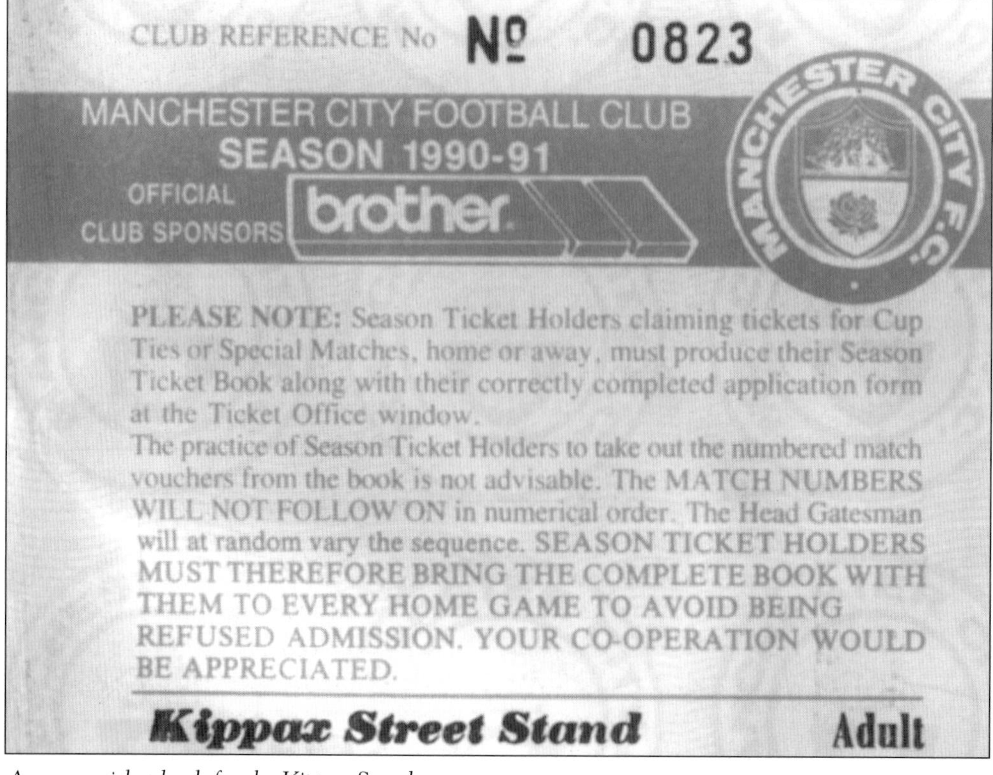
CLUB REFERENCE No Nº 0823

MANCHESTER CITY FOOTBALL CLUB
SEASON 1990-91
OFFICIAL CLUB SPONSORS brother

PLEASE NOTE: Season Ticket Holders claiming tickets for Cup Ties or Special Matches, home or away, must produce their Season Ticket Book along with their correctly completed application form at the Ticket Office window.
The practice of Season Ticket Holders to take out the numbered match vouchers from the book is not advisable. The MATCH NUMBERS WILL NOT FOLLOW ON in numerical order. The Head Gatesman will at random vary the sequence. SEASON TICKET HOLDERS MUST THEREFORE BRING THE COMPLETE BOOK WITH THEM TO EVERY HOME GAME TO AVOID BEING REFUSED ADMISSION. YOUR CO-OPERATION WOULD BE APPRECIATED.

Kippax Street Stand **Adult**

A season ticket book for the Kippax Stand.

Left: *Rodney Marsh was an unpredictable genius, who produced some marvellous goals for City.* Right: *Tommy Caton joined City as a junior in 1978. He died of a suspected heart attack in April 1993, at the age of thirty.*

was eleven and a youth soccer player, so I quickly got interested in the English League. So what if I'd never heard of any of these teams or the players or the British terminology? It became an obsession, waiting for the Thursday delivery of a new *Shoot* to the local newsagent. One problem, though. I had to pick a team. How? Who? I had no allegiance to any sector of the land. Liverpool was an obvious choice, since they were employing an Israeli full-back named Avi Cohen at the time. Right off, I knew I hated United. But, for some reason, I was drawn to the strip on the back cover of that first issue. The late, great Tommy Caton in light blue. And there you have it. I came home a City fan – for life. Of course, there wasn't much City info waiting for me. Internet access, cable TV, or even a newsstand that would import magazines from the UK were all years away. For a good decade, *Shoot* was all I knew, the copies that my relatives mailed me from Israel and, ultimately, an expensive subscription my uncle arranged during my senior year of high school. Thankfully though, through technology, I've been able to follow City much closer the last five years. Various sports channels have been running the Premiership's one-hour highlight show since about 1990 (as far as I know). Cyberspace provides more

The programme from the League Cup semi-final, second leg, against Middlesbrough.

reading material than I could want. And Los Angeles, with so many transplanted Brits, features several pubs that show matches live on satellite for $5 to $10 – albeit Newcastle and United – every week.

Marc Stein

Well, it all began on 21 January 1976 – City against Middlesbrough in the League Cup semi-final, second leg. I was squashed into the Kippax Stand with some of the other members of the Openshaw branch of the City Supporters' Club. Result? 4-0! We all know the consequences of that excellent evening, a night that changed my life forever! Then Wembley, and Dennis Tueart's unforgettable goal! (Twenty-four years later, and he signed the Wembley '76 programme I kept, where his photograph has slightly more hair, his words!) Thanks for that memory and autograph, Dennis, or should I say Mr Tueart nowadays? City have been in my blood, Blue blood, ever since! I can't explain why, but I love you City, I do! I'm sure you all understand how I feel. It's the supporters and the atmosphere, I need that buzz, that fix! I will support Manchester City for the rest of my life, because I am a proper Manc! Twenty-four years of MCFC, the highs, the lows. The recent and much needed (and dreamed of) successes (most notably, at Wembley in 1999 and the 4-1 win over Blackburn); Moonchester – nearly ejected at Wolves away two seasons ago, nightmare game football, isn't it? Jumpers for goalposts! The most loyal fans in the universe! City 'til I die!

Mark Redgrave

In 1955, there was only one house in our street in Swinton with a television, and cars were rarer visitors than the rag and bone man's horse and cart. So, when Mrs Ellis at number forty-six got a TV set, that was where everyone went to watch City in the cup final against Newcastle. I remember nothing of the game itself, except running home crying when Newcastle scored their third goal. It was a suitable introduction to Manchester City.

Ken Corfield

I don't think it's easy to explain why I'm a Blue, I don't suppose anyone consciously picks a team, it sort of picks you. I grew up in Radcliffe, which is between Bolton and Bury, but which didn't really feel part of either footballing town to me. My Dad worked as a (thin) controller for British Rail in Manchester, which meant I felt more allegiance to the big city. I've always had a sense of humour, despised 'big heads', preferred blue and have been proud of the City of Manchester, having also been born there (at St Mary's Hospital, now a new complex of flats, opposite the Palace Theatre). I could only support Manchester City, couldn't I? My first match was as a ten-year-old, when I was lucky enough to see City beat the German side Schalke 04 in the semi-final second leg of the European Cup-winners' Cup (5-1). It was a never-to-be-forgotten experience. My Mum was born in Gelsenkirchen, Germany, home of Schalke, which was the reason I was allowed to go to this game. My uncle was a tour guide for a party of Schalke fans. I didn't care! I was only bothered about seeing my heroes, and fittingly, my all-time favourite player, Colin Bell, scored. The thing that surprised me was the colour of the occasion. It was a night match, so outside it was a grey and dismal April evening, people dressed in dull colours, tired and hunched over. From the outside, the ground looked old, tired and in desperate need of a makeover, even I could see that as a ten-year-old! Once inside though, there was an explosion of colour, noise and raw excitement. I'd never seen anything like it. I was supposed to be excited about seeing my uncle, but I hardly noticed him in the fifteen minutes it seemed to take, for the ninety minutes to flash back. I can remember shouts for Nellie Young, and my mum having some banter with City fans, who'd worked out she was German. Already the good humour was evident. I was already

The players begin their celebrations after clinching promotion.

This vehicle has raised a few eyebrows in the Tameside area!

a Blue by the time I attended that match, but that first game confirmed my commitment for life. I've made sacrifices along the way, to watch my beloved Blues. I left Manchester at the age of eighteen to attend Sunderland Polytechnic on a three-year degree course – it lasted three weeks! I couldn't cope with the thought of travelling all over the place from Sunderland to see my team play. In that brief time in Sunderland, I remember attending a mid-week League Cup tie at Blackpool, leaving after an afternoon lecture at the poly to return at 6.00 a.m. the following day, after sitting on Leeds station all night, waiting for a connection back to Sunderland. My best friend asked me to be best man at his wedding on Saturday in the 1980s; I politely declined, preferring to watch City against Birmingham. I think we lost! Most embarrassingly, while a steward on the Supporters' Club Football Specials of the 1970s and '80s; I missed the train back from Southampton. I'd arrived back at the station from the match nice and early, in the company of Supporter's Club secretary Frank Horrocks and my dad (British Rail employee!). The three of us asked which platform the train was to return from, and duly headed to the quiet end of the station. The police convoy bringing the rest of the fans must have lined up outside the station as quiet as church mice, to eventually be led onto a different platform from ours to board the train, which then silently slid away on its return journey to Manchester. My dad, Frank and I sat there, oblivious! Eventually we wondered where everyone was, only to find out they'd been and gone. The three-change journey home, and following months, was highly embarrassing, to say the least! It took a very long time indeed to live it down.

Ian Cheeseman

I have supported City for over thirty years and have always been proud to be Blue, advertising the fact by displaying the club crest pennants dangling from the mirror in my car and van. I had just picked up my new van (blue, of course) from the garage and was driving to the sign writers, when I realised that I had left my pennant in my old van, that I had just traded in. Then the idea came to me that whilst he was putting my company logo on the side of the van, that he could put the club crest on the bonnet. Now while driving around Manchester, fellow Blues sound their horns in appreciation, and when the van is parked, people actually stop and stare at it with a smile on their faces. I have displayed the crest for over a year, and it has not been damaged in any way.

Brian Prendergast

CHAPTER 7
The Best Of Times

The programme from the game against Huddersfield which set a club record for the highest-scoring victory.

White Van

It was Tuesday 22 March 1977, and I had the day off. City were away that evening to QPR (kick-off, 7.30 p.m.) and no one I knew was going. We were third in the League, behind Liverpool and Ipswich Town, with thirty-nine points – four points above United who were fourth. I decided to go at the last minute, and went to Maine Road to see if I could get on a Supporters' Club coach. They were all full, but some guys in a white Escort van offered me a lift, so I was on my way. We arrived in London, which in those days was a very dodgy venue indeed, and stories were flying around that Chelsea, Millwall and every other nutter in London would be looking for Mancs. I knew that QPR had no 'Boys', so thought that it would be OK and these stories were pure fantasy. How wrong I was! We parked the van near White City, and I remember walking past The Springbok pub, which is still there today, twenty-four years later. No trouble outside, and so we went into the old open-end terracing. There were about fifty or so Blues, who were anticipating trouble. There were some of the usual 'Heads' about, who loved kicking off, and it did not take long as segregation was completely non existent, which was common then. There was also zero police presence – well, maybe one who would quickly disappear at the first sign of bother. A group of fans arrived from under the side stand and were strangely chanting 'Chelsea!' We had to fight with our backs to the wall and actually chased them off. We felt safe now, and this group of Blues stayed together for the rest of the match until the end of the game, which ended 0-0. At the end of the match, all the Blues split and it was every man for himself. There were Cockneys everywhere outside the ground shouting 'Do the Northern *!?@#*'. I walked towards White City, trying to mingle and find the white Escort van. My plan failed and I felt a push from behind, which I ignored, and then I was kicked, and my heart was racing like the clappers. I thought 'I have got to do something', so I quickly turned around to see a crew of about ten, with the main one brandishing a blade. My life passed before me, but I thought very quickly and said in the best Cockney accent I could 'What's your f*!@?#g problem?' 'What's your problem?' the knifeman responded. I very nearly said 'Nowt', but quickly changed that to 'Naafin' mate'. He said, 'Yeah, well speak up next time,' and ran off with his crew to look for 'Norverners'. God was I scared, and had nightmares for years about that night. I found the van with the other lads already there. I told them about my ordeal, and they said 'Yeah, yeah'. I don't think they believed me, but it really did happen. Things have changed so much in the last twenty-five years: some good, but loads not so good, especially the costs involved, and I am not sure how much longer I will go to watch my beloved Man City, who I have literally risked my life to support. A real tragedy.

Mark Redgrave

Sports Centre

I didn't have a season ticket in 1987/88, and it was as good as every other game we'd go to. A friend of mine had his thirteenth birthday party that day, so it was decided that I'd go to that instead, even though I did not like him that much. But it was a chance of a game of footy at a sports centre that swayed it. On coming back in the car though, we first heard it was 6-1, and we followed the events from there. Could not believe the final score, and my dad was not too happy and still goes on about it now.

Philip Noble, talking about City's 10-1 victory over Huddersfield

The Bo-Skins

I have seen City play many times at so many different levels, but one of the games I always remember is the first ever pre-season friendly I attended. It was a two-game tour of Germany. Details of what happened are very patchy, but the following is an account of what I can remember. The trip was organized by the MCFC Piccadilly branch of the Supporters' Club. We stocked up with 'tinnies' from an off-licence on Piccadilly Station approach, and got on a train to London. We ended up in Essen in Germany, I'm not sure how, but the obvious route would have been boat and then train. Essen was to be our base, and to get to the match against VFL Bochum, we got another train and went drinking. There were about twenty of us on the trip and we split up. Me, my mate Trevor and a couple of others went into a traditional Bierkeller, where I had my first-ever taste of strong German lager. We then had to find the ground and started to walk down a road with a grass hill along one side. This was where we met the 'Bo-Skins' for the first time, as they came charging down the hill, thinking we were typical English soccer hooligans. Needless to say, we found our way to the ground a lot quicker than expected. In the ground, we stood behind the goals, and marvelled at the warm-up skills of David 'Psycho' Cross, who had just signed for City. We were soon joined by several other Blues and the 'Bo-Skins' again, who were now offering people fights on a one-to-one basis. None of us took up their kind offer, as we slowly mingled into the crowd. I cannot remember very much about the game. I think City won, and the only other part of the trip I remember, is being at the train station after the match. Waiting to go back to Essen, and rumours were circulating that the 'Bo-Skins' were about to charge the platform. Then, all of a sudden, we heard this bawling and shouting, and thought this must be them coming, only to find that Helen 'The Bell' Turner was scaring them all off. It was funny at the time.

Andrew Thomas

Helen 'The Bell' Turner, one of City's most extrovert supporters.

Last Train To Newcastle

Away trips, I have made a few. I went to Derby in '72, I think we got beat 4-0, and after the game, there were several thousand City fans being police-marched to the train station, when it went off because a few Derby fans were throwing bricks at us. The police lost the plot as usual and started to wade into us; my pal and I were on a street corner when the horses charged, all I heard was my pal say: 'that horse is coming straight at meeeeeeeee'. When I next looked, I saw him dripping from the front of the horse about fifty yards down the street. I do remember saying 'move', but he couldn't've heard me. Villa park in 1981. 1-0, Paul Power free-kick I don't remember much after that, it was just a wild frenzy of pure ecstasy. What I do remember is arriving back in Piccadilly Station on a train of some 1,200 or so City fans and having bottles thrown at us from the top of a bridge by about twenty Chelsea fans, who had been at Oldham, and the police pleading with City fans not to react, while they let the dogs loose on the Chelsea fans. Wild scenes, but we were at Wembley to play Spurs, and look where that got us. I went to both games, and on the Friday stood outside Maine Road to welcome back the team, about 1,000 there, and Gerry Gow and Tommy Hutchinson walked around everyone shaking hands and apologizing for losing. That made being a Blue even more important, the passion and feeling, you went away with left a bigger feeling and lump in the throat than had we won. It was a similar thing in '74, when we had lost to Wolves in the League Cup final. Our fans were incredible, the scenes outside Wembley and at Euston Station were as if we had won and not Wolves. Being part of all that really begins to tell the story of why I stay a Blue and do not go chasing glory with other clubs who win consistently. It might not always be fashionable to be Blue, but even when it gets hard it is still etched in your blood from so many great memories. Arsenal away, 1971 – what a day to remember. All started well down on the train: myself and my best pal, Glyn – we have been pals now for almost thirty-five years, and in that time have experienced almost every high and low you can imagine in football. Anyway, went down with a gang we met on the train, so there were about twelve of us, got to Highbury on the Tube, first pub we went in was full of Arsenal fans, so we made a quick exit from there. Finally found a pub, then went to the ground. We were in the old Clock End and, to our surprise, found a lot of City fans in there. A few scuffles occurred at the beginning, and in time, we went one down. With fifteen minutes left, we thought that we would leave and get to Euston trouble-free – ha ha! As we got near the exit, about 300 to 400 Arsenal fans came rushing in and all hell broke loose. We ran back into the crowd, only for me to get held by a policeman claiming I had just run in the ground. I kept pleading with him to listen to my accent, but he threw me out. Anyway, my pal had to come with me, as I had the train tickets. So, out on the street at Highbury, right in the middle of a huge group of Arsenal fans, who started to chase us. We managed to lose them, and got on the Tube at Islington. What we did not know was that the Tube went back on itself, and the next call was Highbury. Not too many people got on we thought, but a guy sat opposite and started to moan about how bad the game was. We asked him what the final score was, and he said 2-1 to City. We could hardly hold back our pleasure, but had to, or else get spotted as City fans. Arrived at Euston to find the whole back section of the Tube full of

North Bank idiots, who were trying to single out any accents from Manchester by asking the time etc. I put my head down and legged it for the escalator, but forgot about my pal, who followed several minutes later, a little the worse for wear. By now, there were about twelve of us in the main concourse at Euston, feeling pretty safe and wondering where the main body of City fans were. About 900 of them were nowhere to be seen. Suddenly, a shout went up, and about 200 Arsenal fans came charging out of the Tube area, heading for us. We then all jumped over the platform gate and ran like hell down the platform, pursued by about fifty of the 200 – we did not have many choices. The train on the left was an express to Newcastle, and the train on the right was being cleaned, and the end of the platform was getting nearer and nearer. Decisions had to be made, and we were just about to jump on the Newcastle train when, from nowhere, a police dog-handler appeared and turned the Arsenal fans back. By this time, there were police everywhere, they got us together and were reading us the riot act, when all we had done was a bit of self-preservation. Just then, the police radios kicked in, and it appeared there was a major disturbance down the Tube about 900 City fans running wild with Arsenal fans, so they told us to stay there and off they went. By this time, a large number of Arsenal fans had gathered outside and were coming in dribs and drabs. We realised this, and feeling vulnerable, we mixed in with the crowds. At one point, we were in WHSmith, saying to one another, don't look conspicuous, and then looked at what we were reading and saw it was upside-down and was a girls' magazine! We were never happier than when the main body of City fans arrived – wow, that was some day. One last piece. May '99, and every City fan was at Wembley but us. I had booked a long weekend in York way back, believing that we would not need the play-offs. Picture this: we were at Whitby with our wives and walking around with ear pieces in from our hidden Walkmen, when we noticed people watching us. Then I overheard an old couple talking, they thought we were police on an undercover stakeout. 'Must be drugs', one old dear said to the other, who found this quite amusing. At 2-0 down, I thought it was all over, so we went into a café for a coffee. My pal then jumped up and said Horlock had scored. I still thought 'no chance', but when a bowl of sugar flew in the air and over me, we rushed out dancing much to the embarrassment of our wives and the amusement of the locals, who had no idea what was going on. Tension? It could not've been worse if we had been there. Walking up Whitby pier listening to the penalties was a nightmare, and then it was all over and we were completely going barmy, when some old dear walked past our wives and said it must be bloody football.

Mike Ash

The Times

Divorces! I got divorced on the strength of my love for City, but we will not go into that, because it's already been covered in the *Times*. The best party has got to be Blackburn away the season before last, one of the best days out. It's a ten-day drinking session following City that sticks in my mind. I am not a drinker generally, but it was Tranmere at home on the Saturday, a full-day session. We were at Portsmouth on the Monday, so we travelled down on the Sunday and I got blind drunk that evening. I can't remember much of the night, not even the picture that appears in the fanzine *Bert Trautmann's*

Helmet. I was drinking cider all night with the fanzine boys, and I was unconscious on the floor by the end of the night. Then came the Birmingham game on the Friday – another full day session. We started at 11.00 a.m. and finished at 11.00 p.m. That was another good day too; I was in better condition that day, because it was spread over a period of time.

Tom Ritchie

Cheese 'n' Onion Pie

Once, on a trip to Burnden Park, we went down on the train and had arranged to meet some friends in a pub. I had not seen the sign over the door, which said 'No away fans'. So, when the massive doorman asked me where was I from, I immediately said 'Manchester', and he retorted 'Well, you're not coming in here then', so we were stuck, but eventually ended up in GM Buses' Social Club. That was only the beginning of our troubles; our tickets were with our friends in the other pub. So, we decided to split up and try and get into our original destination, and somehow it worked. The next problem was our tickets. They were for the home end, so about eight of us – including 'Eike', so named because he was the spitting image of City's 'keeper at the time, Eike Immel – went into the Lions' Den and mingled freely, but remained very quiet, until I made the mistake of asking somebody in my Mancunian accent where he got his cheese and onion pie from – only a home supporter would have

The party begins. Supporters begin to gather outside Maine Road, after hearing the news that City had beaten Blackburn Rovers 4-1 to gain promotion.

known that, and the pie hut was just to the right of me, so I had given the game away. Fortunately, nothing happened, but we were watching our backs for the rest of the game.

Seamus McAndrew

Mr Hanbury

The first-ever game I went to was on a school trip. It was against Wolves at home, in 1978, the days of Kenny Hibbert and George Berry. Our school – St Catherine's in Didsbury – got tickets for the North Stand. We were in the third or fourth year, about nine or ten years old. Mr Hanbury used to get free tickets for the school, but to actually get the tickets at school you had to be in the choir.

Paul Mitchell

The Quiz

I will always remember a trip on the Travel Club train to Bournemouth. The author of this book set a quiz, and I won it. There were quite a few people in it and all had paid a pound. I think I won about £25 to £30, which was quite a bit of money at that time. I was doing the quiz whilst selling food from the tuck shop.

Steve Boyd

Sex Orgy

The football world reeled one season with the revelations of a wild sex orgy at a reserve game against Coventry City. Picture the scene: May Day (and it was, for one of the participants). The Blues cruising along nicely, two up, thanks to a first-minute Wayne Clarke penalty and an own goal. Nothing to get excited about … then, it happened. A titter bubbled up in one area, a giggle burst from another; the City groupies shrieked and people looked around, wondering why the tranquility was suddenly shattered. Gradually, eyes focused on the rampant orgy taking place on the touchline. Three ducks from Platt Fields Lake had decided that a spot of congress would liven things up for the spectators. Male number one fluttered and shifted about, finding a comfy position, the female shuffled and wriggled, eager to accommodate his every desire. Male number two stood to one side, awaiting his tern (sorry, turn), licking his beak in anticipation. Off they went, cheered on by a vast crowd of around 600. Never mind the thrust of the Blues forwards, male number one provided plenty of his own, as he pursued his role of increasing the Platt Fields duck population. By now the game was forgotten, as the al fresco humpty-dumpty became the total centre of attention. Players started to look puzzled at the spasmodic bursts of applause for nothing more than a safe back-pass. End of Act One. Male number one fell off; preened himself, then, together with his mate and male number two, waddled towards the edge of the penalty area. Clearly encouraged by the fans' appreciation, male number two then climbed aboard and proceeded to try to affect the parts other ducks cannot reach. The ball went out of play. The ref, obviously worried by the lax moral standards on display, ran across and, together with a linesman and the Coventry 'keeper, tried to shoo the insatiable fowl away. A most unwise decision – a storm of booing broke around the heads of the interfering trio, and a cry from the top of the

Maine Stand: 'Leave them alone. How would you like it if you had not finished?' Any official worth his whistle would have fished out a red card. For what reason? Fowl and abusive language, perhaps, or persistent misconducked! He contented himself with timing the birds with his stopwatch, and soon male number two climbed off and smirked at the still-recovering male number one. Somehow, all three found the energy to swagger towards the halfway line, then as one, they took off in perfect formation, banked, and headed back to Platt Fields, over the Kippax roof, to bursts of applause from the audience.

John Maddocks

Steve Daley – fear outweighed his ability and, with hindsight, the purchase of Daley should never have happened.

Funniest Moments

I think we all need cheering up. Even though many of the incidents listed were not funny at the time, the sands of time (and pints of lager) have passed, and they do now appear to tickle the funny bone. Our much-patented gallows humour has served us well. I even remember in one of the fanzines they ran a competition for readers to select City's worst-ever line-up. In the first fanzine of the new season, the author stated that, sadly, there were so many entries, it completely ruined his summer holiday sifting through so many interlopers, such as Brannan, Creaney, Sugrue, Biggins, Daley – oh, the list is endless! In no particular order and off the top of my head:

– The Hutchison own goal in the '81 FA Cup final.

– Alan Ball: 'Play the ball to the corner, lads, we only need a draw to avoid relegation'.

– The ironic reversal in fortunes of both Manchester clubs after the '5-1'.

– Man City break UK transfer record by signing Steve Daley for £1.5m.

– City sign Stockport ace, headline in the *Manchester Evening News*, c. 1978.

– The 'Forward (and then "down") with Franny' campaign.

– Steve 'I'm here for the long haul' Coppell (thirty-three days, actually).

– Five managers in the space of six weeks, and virtually every pub quiz in the North West covered this subject in the sports section, even the joke about having a 'manager who lasts a month' competition.

– I did hear a story that the editor of the City fanzine *Electric Blue* was threatened with court action by the owners of a pornographic magazine of the same name, for misuse of a copyright name that potentially besmirches the good name of their publication.

– The David Pleat jig on the pitch was perhaps one of the cruellest.
– City conceded a penalty and the pitch was so muddied up the penalty spot had disappeared. The striker (I forget his name) placed the ball where he thought it should be. Joe Corrigan picked up the ball and said it wasn't there, and began pacing out where the penalty spot should be. Big Joe got booked and then the player scored.
– 30,000 people appearing at Maine Road on a Friday evening to see Swales booted out of office, thinking that the new man was going to be our saviour.
– Swales had an altercation with F.H. Lee in 1973, and he promptly transfer-listed and sold him, and then Lee said. 'You will regret this decision, as I will come back to haunt you one day'. Lee went on to win the League with Derby and scored the winner against us at Maine Road on his first return. I remember Barry Davies (I think) on *Match Of The Day*, saying 'just look at Francis Lee's face', as Derby took the two points (as it was then) back to the Baseball Ground (as it was then), and promptly won the league and gave F.H. Lee his only League Championship medal. That's when I knew being a City fan was going to be painful.
– It was a glorious day, the sun was shining and City, with their deep-rooted ties with the community, opened their family stand – the bit between the Maine Stand and the North Stand. Trevor Francis recorded a soundbyte on Piccadilly Radio (as it was then) hailing this as a great day for the club: two adults with two children, then one of the kids gets in free (I forget the exact concession). 'No swearing' posters, plenty of stewards, application forms to join Junior Blues, sweets, no booze in this stand etc. – joy upon joy. Late in the second half, Big Trev was fouled on one of his runs by a terrible challenge, right in front of the family stand. High-pitched boos echoed from the pre-pubescent youngsters (our kid and me included) who saw their hero, Trev, clatter to the ground. Trev gets up, remonstrates with the assailant, a few handbags exchanged, and Trev headbutts him on the hooter in classic style. The bloodied assailant gets up, looking like an extra from *Reservoir Dogs*. Trev is turning on the showers before the red card is put back into the pocket, and he can't even manage a wave to the adoring lads and lasses in the uncovered section of the family stand, after giving an 'R'-rated performance.
– Being at Wolves, getting hammered 3 0 at half-time, an awful night. During the second half (I think we were 4-0 down by then), the crowd pipes up: 'John Bond, John Bond give us a wave, John Bond, give us a wave'. The blond pretender waits for a moment, we give him another chorus, and he looks to the away end and gives us a half-hearted wave. In unison, like some mass neurosis had overtaken all of us, the entire City contingent in the

The Junior Blues are reputed to have the largest membership in the country for a junior organization.

Andy Dibble was embarrassed at being hoodwinked by Gary Crosby of Nottingham Forest. The incident once appeared on the BBC's A Question of Sport *in the 'What happened next?' round.*

away end were on the same wavelength, and in some Pavlovian reaction, we all leaned forward, two fingers rampant in 'V' formation, and screamed at the top of our lungs a two-word offensive phrase connected with sex and travel.

– Unforgettable incident at Nottingham Forest, when Crosby receiving treatment behind Dibble's goal ran back on to the pitch, after several life-saving dabs of the magic sponge, he crept up behind Dibble who had the ball on the palm of his hand, ready to kick out, nudged it out of his hand and scored. You can hear David Coleman: 'err, what happened next Emlyn?' for years to come.

– Quinn scores, and we take the lead. Our goalie, Tony Coton, brings down a Derby player in the box. Penalty. This would have equalized the game. Quinny saves: 'Ireland's, Ireland's Number One'.

– Away at the Dell. Saints fans singing 'You will never see our new ground', and the lads retorting 'You will never fill your ground'.

– Kevin Bond was still fairly new to the club, had not won over large sections of the crowd, and was getting the 'daddy's boy' chant from both sets of fans at Maine Road. His dedication was like that of Paul Dickov and Neil McNab put together, the crowd favourite. However, Nicky Reid (did he ever score?) couldn't put a foot wrong, but had nowhere near the same level of commitment as young Kev. A little off-form one day, the crowd was getting restless, and I think we were 1-0 down. Young Kev picks up the ball thirty to thirty-five yards out, nudges it to his left, sidesteps a potential defender, the ball hits a raised divot and takes the sweetest of bounces to raise it four or five inches off the ground. Young Kev leans over the ball, text-book style, and sweeps his left foot in a Tiger Woods golf swing through the nicely teed-up object, and the ball arcs majestically through the air, and at the end of the projectile's path, the ball is nestling in the back of the net, after the despairing efforts of the goalkeeper, who slumped in a crumpled heap by the right-hand post. The goal was a sheer dream, any other player, any other team, and we would be seeing it *ad nauseum* on footy shows for years to come. Kevin Bond turned

Left: *Niall Quinn, who both scored the winner and saved a penalty against Derby.* Right: *Nick Reid, the crowd's favourite – a product of City's fine youth policy in the 1970s. He made a total of 256 League and 7 Cup appearances, before moving to Blackburn Rovers in July 1987.*

towards the Kippax, arms out in crucifix-fashion, as if to say: 'What do you think of that, now will you accept me?' It was one of the most beautiful goals I have ever seen at Maine Road, especially when viewed from the North Stand. Fair play, Kevin Bond.

Those are some of the best, as I witnessed them, but I know there will be others. However, for far and away the funniest and most classic moment in Man City's history, we take you back to a warm and sunny Old Trafford, in the spring of April 1974. The pictures are brought to you by Granada TV, and the commentary is provided by the dulcet tones of a certain middle-aged moustachioed gentleman. The incident was catastrophic in its outcome, but this time, not for the blue half of Manchester.

Roll VT:
Colin Bell, running through the middle of the Old Trafford pitch towards the Stretford End with the ball.
And cue Gerald Sinstadt:
'Here's Bell, Tueart is away on the left, Lee (as he runs into the box, pulling three defenders with him) pulls it across to Law, and Dennis has done it'!

Phil Lines

Going Back

… is the title of a song that I wrote and recorded with a mate of mine back in 1998, and I would like to tell you how and why we wrote it. It all starts back in the 1998/99 season – City are now (for the first time in their history) a Division Two team (the old Third Division). The season started well, with a 3-0 win against Blackpool. Me and my neighbour, Vince Williams (the well-known club singer) have been taking our kids, and other kids from our street, to most matches over the last few seasons and sitting in the Junior Blues section of the North Stand. On our way out of the ground, the old 'Boys in Blue' song was being played, and Vince's son, Kris, asked me what the song was, and I explained to him that I had not heard it for a while, but it was recorded in the early 1970s and was played, for many years, after each match, in the days when City rarely got beat at home. Kris, quick as a flash, replied that it was about time they had a new song, and that me and his dad can sing it. Vince and I thought it was a daft idea, and told him to shut up. City's good start to the season started to turn pear-shaped, and we started losing against teams we should have beaten by cricket scores. The usual jokes about City were doing the rounds again, and the kids we had been taking to the matches were getting fed up. So, Vince suggested that, for a bit of a laugh, we should go along with his son's daft idea and write a song. We discussed what the song should be about, and with City now mid-table in the Division Two, and a lot of supporters losing faith, we decided to use the format of past, present and future – City, once a great team, now relegated from the Premiership; City becoming a great team again and returning to the Premiership – in a kind of a ballad. With some input from myself and the kids, it was not long before Vince had written all the verses. All we had to do then was put the music to it. At the point when we thought things were right, we started getting all the Junior Blues in our street together, and began rehearsing in my house – with thirteen kids in my house, singing at the top of their voices, it did not go down well with my wife, who has spent fifteen years married to me and City, and she hates anything to do with football! It took about ten rehearsals before the kids were singing in harmony, and our next job was to find a recording studio. I was put in touch with Steve Warburton, of SJ Music in Mossley, who was most helpful when we told him what we were doing, and booked us in for a recording. It took about six hours to record the song, as the kids were aged from six to eleven years old, and their voices ranged from high to very high. So, Steve split the kids into three groups and remixed their voices, with me in the background and Vince being the main singer. When it was played back to us, it sounded great, the kids could not believe it was them singing. Steve gave us a few demo tapes, and with the kids all being members of the Junior Blues, I gave them a copy and told them if they liked it, they could maybe sell it at their meetings to raise funds for themselves. The Junior Blues organization loved it, and said they would play it at their next meeting, and also try and get it played prior to the next match at Maine Road. When I told the kids, they were over the moon, and couldn't wait to hear their song played at Maine Road. At the same time, the local *Tameside Reporter* newspaper got involved with the story and did a full-page feature on us. This is where our problems started. We all turned up at the next Junior Blues meeting at the Odeon cinema in Manchester, and were told the song could not be played, as the cinema did not have facilities to play CDs or tapes, and that the song would not be played at Maine Road. When I broke the news to the kids, they were very disappointed, and seeing the look on their faces at being let down, I decided to do something myself. During the JB's meeting, I explained the situation to the cinema manager, and he introduced me to the projectionist, who put the tape into his

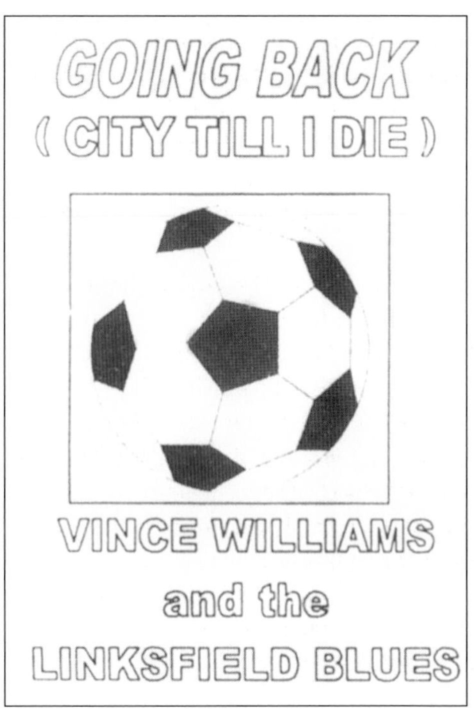

Cassette cover from the City song 'Going Back'.

machine and played it at the end of the meeting. Immediately, parents of JB's were asking what the song was and is it on sale. Due to the good response, the following week, I distributed it to a few local Supporters' Clubs for them to play at meetings, again the response was good and I got quite a few orders. So, I went and got 500 copies recorded on tape and CD and officially released the song. I tried City again, but the answer was still 'No'. One thing I have learnt over the past 30 years supporting City, is never give up, so I decided to promote the record myself. I dropped copies off to all local radio stations, got in touch with the local paper that had carried the first article. They printed a further article with the opening text: 'The song that has been barred from Maine Road'. After this article was pub-

PLEASED: the singing youngsters with (l-r) Kent O'Sullivan, Vince Williams and Brian Prendergast (CD98-1080)

Young fans over the blue moon

by NICK HULME

A GROUP of young Manchester City fans was over the blue moon when the chance to perform its own musical tribute to the team on the hallowed turf of Maine Road appeared.

Blues balmy Brian Prendergast,36, from Linksfield, Denton, led the 13 youngsters onto the pitch before City's game against Notts County last week.

The performance of the original song 'Going Back - City Till I Die' marked the end of a long struggle for Brian and the children.

A life-long City fan who once went to see the team play on his wedding day, Brian had campaigned long and hard to get the song played at Maine Road since it was recorded in November last year.

Originally, the club said they couldn't play it, because they were contractually obliged to only play music that featured on the Piccadilly Key 103 playlist.

But Brian's persistence finally paid off. Nearly five months after the song was written, the young fans finally realized their dream.

Brian revealed: "All the kids had a great time. We were led straight past all the queues and through the player's tunnel onto the pitch. There were about 26,000 at that game. They played the song and we all took a bow.

"We're all really pleased that the song was finally played at Maine Road. It's what we wanted all along."

The song is now being sold at an unofficial City merchandise shop on Maine Road, and has shifted over 280 copies.

It has also been played regularly at Hyde United's ground, home of City's reserve team.

Brian even believes the success of the song may be in some way responsible for City's recent winning run.

He explained: "Since the record came out the team have really been on a roll, and they've only lost one game. It may have given them an extra boost, who knows?"

He added: "If they get promotion this season, we might even consider doing a follow-up single."

A report on the song, taken from the Tameside Reporter, *March 1999.*

lished, the publicity took off. We were invited onto Greater Manchester Radio to do a show; we were invited on Granada Tonight, where we sang the song. We were also contacted by a few other newspapers and ended up on the front page of the *Stockport Times*, in a half-page article in the *Manchester Evening News*, and in a photo in the City magazine, as well as all the City fanzines. Hyde United also requested a CD, so they could play it at City reserve matches. The tapes and CDs were also sold at the Soccer Shop (corner of Maine Road). By this time, the kids thought they were celebrities, appearing on TV, radio, and having their photos in newspapers, but they still had not got what they had been promised, that the song would be played at Maine Road. I contacted a number of people associated with the club, to see what they could do. It must have worked, because I got a call from the club, and a week later, a letter arrived, inviting us all to a match, and it explained that the song would be played before the game, and that we could come onto the pitch and take a bow. It was a great night for the kids, hearing their song played at Maine Road. The day after, the *Tameside Reporter* ran a front-page article of our success. So to sum up – when Kris had the idea of releasing a record about City, they were mid-table in Division Two. When I released the record, City had just started a winning run, and by the time it was played at Maine Road, City were going for a place in the play-offs. That season, City did reach the play-off final, and beat Gillingham to be promoted to Division One. A year later, we were promoted again, beating Blackburn Rovers to go back into the Premier League – back where we belong! Was our song 'Going Back' an omen?

Brian Prendergast

What Happened Next

In all my years of watching football, I have never witnessed anything like the incident I saw at Forest one season. Andy Dibble must have been asleep, as he allowed Crosby to nip out from behind him and nod the ball out of his hands and score. The reaction of the City fans was one of bewilderment; surely the goal could not stand. The goal was not in the spirit of the game. The reaction of Andy Dibble was one of a child who had just lost his favourite toy, stamping his feet and punching the ground. But the goal stood, and even went on to be shown as a clip in the 'What happens next' round on *A Question Of Sport*.

Frank Williams

I Could Write A Book

I first attended Maine Road in April 1956, my Dad used to take me on the crossbar of his pushbike. We beat Sunderland 4-2 that day, and weeks later we won the FA Cup, beating Birmingham City 3-1 at Wembley. I was only nine at the time, and remember running up and down the steps at the back of the Platt Lane Stand, in the area which is now the Family Stand. Maine Road will always hold cherished memories, even though shortly we will be moving to Eastlands, I'll always recall the old green scoreboard and how we all used to gather round waiting for an update on how the first team were doing. It was displayed every fifteen minutes, so the reserve game didn't get too much attention and, for a bit of fun sometimes, the scoreboard attendant put the score up the wrong way, and one particular game – in which we lost 9-2 at West Brom – after

Left: *Billy McAdams joined City from Irish club Distillery in December 1953.* Right: *Paddy Fagan – a versatile, crowd-pleasing winger.*

fifteen minutes we were 2-0 down, we were led to believe it was us winning 2-0. We were all jumping up and down, but the next minute we were groaning – a typical scenario, one would say! Among my most memorable games at Maine Road were Wolves (September 1959, we lost 6-4), Tottenham Hotspur (March 1962, won 6-2), Leicester City (April 1959, won 4-1) – they were just a few to mention. My favourite players included Trautmann, Johnstone, McAdams, Barnes, and Paddy Fagan. During the Joe Mercer-Malcolm Allison glory days, I will not forget the FA Cup tie against Newcastle United on our way to Wembley, where 60,844 spectators packed into Maine Road to see Neil Young and Bobby Owen seal a magnificent victory. I can remember City staging the old FA XI against an Army XI on 7 November 1956: players on view that night were the likes of Bill Leivers, Tom Finney, Jackie Dyson, Eddie Colman, Duncan Edwards, Bobby Charlton and Cliff Jones. I could write a book on all my Maine Road memories and, for me, Joe Mercer was our finest ever manager, Bert Trautmann our finest ever goalkeeper, and Colin Bell? Well, he was simply a footballing gem!

Ted Knott

Citrus And Stripes

In person and on TV, they always let me down, unfortunately. I honestly can't remember them playing a blinder that I could actually watch from start to finish. Sadly, probably the happiest I've ever been leaving a City match was a 1-0 win over Forest, early in the last promotion season. We weren't top of Division One yet, but Kennedy (my new favourite) spun inside City's half and played Goater in for one of Shaun's best-ever finishes. Forest were also expected to be in the promotion fray and I landed in Manchester that morning. So, within six or seven hours, I was at Maine Road watching one of the first hints that we were going to go back up to the Premiership. I still have the video clip of that goal in my computer to remind me of the occasion. Didn't get to watch the Gillingham game because it wasn't televised, but I have my own Gillingham story. Had to follow it over the internet on a five-minute Sporting Life.com score flash from my hotel room in San Antonio, where I was covering the NBA play-offs. When we forced extra time, I couldn't stand the tension any longer and called England. Spent forty-five minutes on the phone with a Manc buddy, who laid the phone next to the TV so I could hear the Sky broadcast. His little boy, now four, to this day says, 'City hit the post, didn't they?' – referring to Dickov's missed penalty in the shootout. I celebrated the triumph by wearing my citrus and stripes kit to NBA media availability between practices for the San Antonio Spurs and Portland Trail Blazers. Kept the shirt on all day and finally went to dinner late that night after finishing work. Got a lot of weird looks from Texans, who had no idea what my bright shirt was all about, but got a huge laugh when I looked up at the TV and saw star Spurs centre David Robinson being interviewed on TV. In the background, there I was, with my bright City shirt glowing in the background. A good day, that one.

Marc Stein

Fancy That

26 December 1988. That date will stick in many people's memories as the day Stoke was invaded by 12,000-plus Man City fans bearing large inflatable bananas, and dressed in a bewildering array of strange fancy dress outfits. One fan described the scenes by saying that although he hadn't had a drink, as he felt light-headed with the atmosphere generated in the ground. It didn't start there though. In the morning, there was a constant stream of traffic on the M6 southbound from Manchester; it seemed that every car had blue scarves flying out of the windows, or contained a rabbit sitting next to Henry VIII or had plastic blow-up bananas on the parcel shelf. One van shot past with bananas stuck to the outside, whilst a taxi arrived at a house in Manchester to be greeted by four gorillas and the muffled words 'Take us to Stoke'. Once in Stoke and that elusive parking spot had been found, it was time to wander round to see what was happening. At the first road junction, three musketeers walked past, complete with swords and frilly hats. A gladiator was munching a hamburger on a street corner and a christmas tree was walking in the general direction of the ground. Every pub in the area was full of strange animals and medieval characters talking, laughing and drinking together – the atmosphere was electric. The Stoke fans seemed rather bemused by the extraordinary sight but were very friendly, whilst even the police joined in and had photographs taken with all sorts of odd-looking characters. Reinforcements must have been called in, as a Canadian Mountie was seen directing the traffic in the middle of the main street. Inside the ground it was packed, despite City fans being given one side and an end. There was plenty to keep me amused, as I waited to

Fancy dress. Frank Newton with his original banana.

greet the team. In the seats behind me was a very official-looking Postman Pat and a Humpty Dumpty who insisted on sitting on the wall. A couple of convicts were nearby; very authentic-looking, right down to the shifty eyes. It was difficult to tell if the policemen sitting near them were real or just City fans in fancy dress. Three dalmations walked by me and continued on past a group of Nazi officers, complete with authentic tunics, peaked caps and long baggy white shorts with swastikas painted on them. When the team arrived, it was as if we had just won the cup, cheering and celebrating as far as the eye could see. The players ran onto the pitch carrying large blow-up bananas, which they threw into the crowd. There were balloons floating in the air, thousands of bananas waving and other weird and wonderful inflatables bobbing up and down in the crowd. The match itself has faded from my memory, partly because we lost, but mainly because there was so much else to take in. The interstellar branch of the City fan club was in evidence, with ET sitting on the fence at half-time; a crocodile and a canary seemed to be getting on intimate terms; whilst I didn't envy the rear half of the pantomime horse wandering round the ground. I wish I had a week or so to walk round the crowd to take in the humour and imagination displayed by the magnificent City following. When the game ended, there was an air of disappointment at the result, but still plenty of laughter, as new delights appeared at every turn of the head. A rather cold-looking fan wandered past wearing a snorkel and flippers and not much else, a group of pixies were spotted heading towards the car park, whilst Rambo, complete with machine gun (with a City scarf tied round it), walked the other way. The following was hailed as the largest mass migration of City fans for a League match since Newcastle in 1968. With the inflatables and fancy dress, I've certainly never seen any thing like it. It was an experience just to be part of the scenes.

Frank Newton

The week on the Isle of Man in 1985, watching City in the Manx tournament was memorable, but during the 1991/92 season, I was in Australia for six months. In the big cities, one live match was shown live each Sunday morning with a 2.00 a.m. kick-off. City's game at Anfield in December was scheduled, so I made the two-hour journey to Sydney. Arriving in the pub screening the game at 8 p.m., and decked out in a City shirt, I soon met up with another Blue who had emigrated a few years back. Of course, by 2.00 a.m. I was completely hammered! There were six Blues there that night, about the same amount of Scousers, and around forty 'Aussie Scousers', mostly of Greek descent. City were a goal down at half-time, but two quick David White lobs put City in front. The six of us went wild! This was too much for the Sky satellite (in its early days then) and the picture was lost for about five minutes. During those long five minutes, I led the singing of 'Blue Moon' booming over Bondi Beach – at 3.00 a.m. – this certainly entertained the locals in the pub waiting until the picture came back! The game finished 2-2, after intense pressure from Liverpool left City hanging on. At 4 a.m., I staggered back to the hostel and slept for about fourteen hours!

Phill Gatenby

One of the best times we ever had, thanks to City, was our holiday in Florida with our friends, the Burgesses. It was announced that City's pre-season tour was to be in Florida. Could we possibly go? For a family who normally holidayed in Llandudno, or Cornwall if we were flush, this was to be a big adventure – but we decided to go for it. On the day we paid up the dosh for this once-in-a-lifetime vacation in a huge Clearwater villa, City decided to cancel the tour. We were gutted. But what the hell, we'd go anyway. We had a brilliant time doing all the usual stuff in the land of big ideas, big steaks and big bums. But more than that, we met up with one of our subscribers, Roger Shore in Tampa, we went to baseball games, and to watch the Tampa Bay Rowdies train – gaining a brilliant interview with Rodney Marsh for the next season's *King of the Kippax*. Best of all was just spending so much time talking about City with great friends. In the end we were glad City hadn't made it, the results just might have put a dampener on the proceedings.

Dave Wallace

My favourite game of all-time was Ipswich Town away in the 1981 FA Cup semi-final. It was not just the game; it was what it meant. I had been to the League Cup Final in 1976, Wolves in 1974; great times, but to get to the FA Cup Final in the centenary season ... I was with all my mates that day, that made it special and there were three carloads of us.

All in the pub by 11.00 a.m., I must admit, I was in tears when Paul Power scored. I knew we were through, I knew what it meant.

Tom Ritchie

When I was a very young kid, we beat Newcastle United 4-3 to win the League Championship. I was only fifteen then, and things did pass me by a bit, but that has to be the greatest game overall, because you don't know if we will ever win it again.

Steve Boyd

City were looking for just one point from their final game of the season at Bradford to gain automatic promotion. On the day of the game we set off very early, hoping to beat the traffic on the M62, but some wise person decided that some of the white lines need touching up and, after what seemed an eternity, we finally reached Bradford after negotiating the roadworks. Parked up and went through the police cordon and ticket check and into the ground. The first thing that struck us was that Blues were not just packed in behind the goal, but they were in the main stand and, what appeared to be, quite a large proportion of the other end of the ground. Bradford went one up after about twenty minutes and that was how it remained at the interval. There was some tremendous pressure from City in the second half, with all sorts of rumours floating around about how Crystal Palace were doing (the only team that had any realistic chance of denying us promotion). Then this long-haired figure raced onto the pitch and went up to various players, telling them that Palace were winning. If that was not enough incentive for the players to get the point we desperately needed, we carried on pressing, and after missing loads of chances, the goal eventually came from Trevor Morley. When the final whistle went, the police and stewards showed a touch of common sense and opened the gates to allow us to pour onto the pitch to congratulate our heroes. I suppose most will say the 5-1 in 1989, but for me, it was the 10-1 against Huddersfield in 1987. Ten goals, three hat-tricks, and the ref awarding Town a penalty out of sympathy – scored by ex-Blue Andy May. When White went round the 'keeper, the emotions of witnessing what could be a tenth goal was unbelievable, and as he slotted the ball home, the crowd just erupted into ecstasy.

Phill Gatenby

The 1956 FA Cup final on telly, and then the 5-4 win at home to Chelsea. 2-0 down at half-time, when my mate Jack told me not to worry (he introduced himself to me at Maine Road last season). We pulled back to 2-2, and then it was 2-3, 3-3, 3-4, 4-4, and finally 5-4. A hat-trick for Bobby Johnstone and two from Joe Hayes. Biggest miss was the 8-1 *v.* Scunthorpe at Christmas 1963, when as a lazy teenager, I overslept. Obviously, there was the ballet-on-ice game *v.* Spurs in the Championship season; the 4-3 title-clincher at Newcastle, but too tense to be enjoyable. The Wembley wins; 5-1 *v.* Schalke; any win *v.* United; the 10-1 *v.* Huddersfield; the Charlton 5-1 promotion game; Stoke fancy dress day; the Bradford 1-1 promotion game; the Gillingham play-off final; and the Blackburn promotion-clincher – how did we do it?

Dave Wallace

CHAPTER 8
The Fanzines

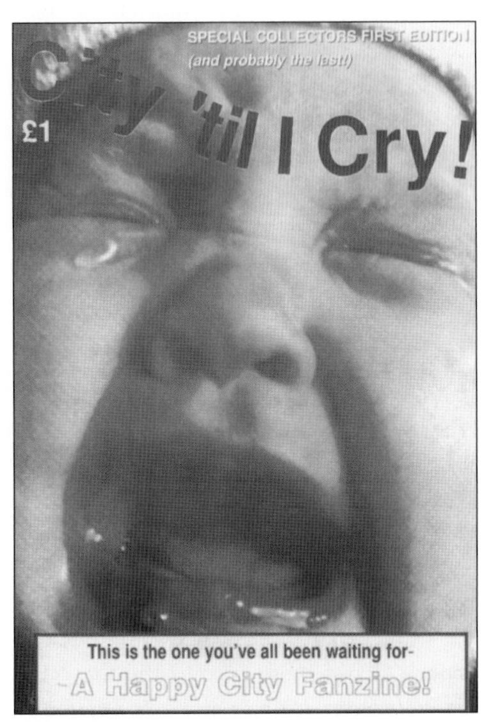

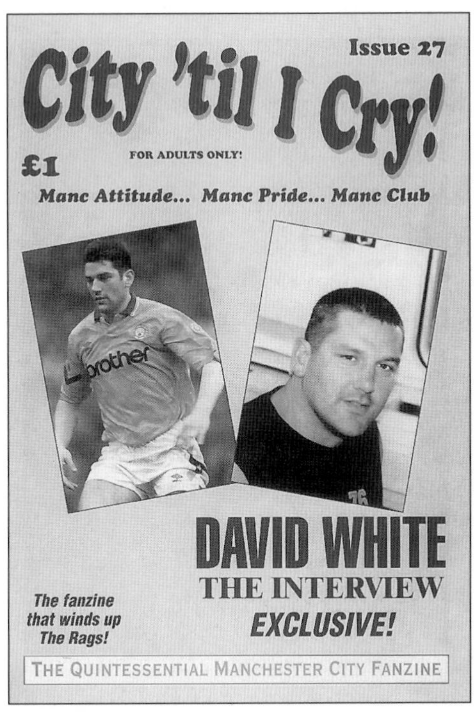

Left: *The very first issue of* City 'Til I Cry. Right: *A recent issue of* City 'Til I Cry *– the quintessential fanzine is still going strong.*

City 'Til I Cry

The fanzine was, in all practical terms, probably conceived just hours after the embarrassing demise of City at the Britannia Stadium with their drop into Division Two. In spite of a thumping 5-2 victory, there were lots of things I wanted to say, and not enough space to fit them all in! Having been a contributor to both *King of the Kippax* and *Bert Trautmann's Helmet* (*née Electric Blue*) for the previous seven or eight years, I was well versed in spouting bile and bitterness ... but writing a couple of articles a month simply wasn't going to suffice … I could have filled a book with my views on City at that time! Over the years, a few mates and I had always hinted at the idea of producing a fanzine, with the monies generated to be used to pay for curry meals on Wilmslow Road. Ah, the innocence of youth! But as City fell to their lowest point ever, my frustrations with the current City fanzines, and their inability to satisfy my cravings to espouse my ever-increasing anger, brought me to the eventual decision to go my own way. The first issue had a picture of a crying baby on the front cover, to represent my own personal feelings at the time about my beloved City. And the title *City 'til I cry!*, a play on the words of the most popular City song at the time, 'City 'til I die'. And believe me, City brought me to tears on far too many occasions. Even though there were numerous times when it was tears of joy rather than sorrow. But you get my drift. We started to sell the very first issue in July 1998, and, if I remember correctly, it was at a reserve-team friendly at mighty Droylsden. I remember thinking to myself that no one would buy a copy, and the first time I exchanged a copy of my fanzine for a shiny £1 coin, I felt like I was the new Rupert Murdoch. The first issue actually sold out, and copies are very rare. That could have been that. I had done what I wanted to do, get a fanzine out in my name, it had sold, it had been generally well received (apart from a less-than-generous review from *King of the Kippax*) and I had made my mark as a City fan. But I felt that it was a bit of a cop-out to bring just the one issue out. I had seen so many fanzines in the past come out for a couple of issues, before sliding back into anonymity, and I was keen that mine would not be seen in such a flippant manner. So if I was to continue, I had to take it seriously. When issues two and three hit the streets, both sold well; I was getting many nice compliments about it being 'different' from what else was on offer, and the egotist in me lapped it up. Trust me, every fanzine editor, no matter what team they follow, has the ego the size of a small eastern European state when it comes to being opinionated. Doing a fanzine is truly a labour of love, there's no money in it, really. Just enough to pay for away matches and the odd pint (and a biryani on Wilmslow Road), but compared to the work you have to put in, its almost slave labour rates. I suppose the great satisfaction I get from the fanzine (apart from bagging up all the pound coins on a Saturday night) is the creative side: writing, layout, receiving some tremendous articles from the hardy bunch of regular contributors, putting it all together. Then that magical moment when the boxes arrive from the printers and you pack up all the copies, ready for selling. The first issue I received from the printers was almost like seeing the birth of your first child. Looking down on hundreds of copies of a product that *you* designed and created. Almost makes it all worthwhile. On the dark side of the equation. Stood in the freezing cold when it's chucking it down with rain, fed up, getting abuse from some small-town no-mark, struggling to convince anyone to buy a copy. Trust me, there have been numerous times when I have vowed 'enough is enough'. Then there is getting in five minutes after the match starts, or leaving a couple of minutes before the end. The crushing in the concourse at half-time, humping a huge bag around. Aye, it's a man's life in fanzine world. The purpose of the fanzine when it started was fairly simple. First, I needed an outlet for my views on City, as doing articles for other 'zines could not suffice. I had become a bit obsessive about City, and the chance to air my somewhat opinionated views had assumed far too great an importance for me, on a personal level. The chance to write down my feelings became almost therapeutic, and even though the team may have been struggling, the 'zine gave me the opportunity to enjoy the football culture without the results being the be-all and end-all of my existence. I could become a bit more 'philosophical' about my support of City; a bit more objective and less tied to their results. The fanzine allowed me to detach myself, to a degree, from the machinations of the team, allowing me to enjoy the 'day' more. Even when City lost, I could, at least, have something else to worry about rather than over-concerning myself with the performance of those representing me. Secondly, it had clearly become a matter of pride. I wanted the fanzine to improve, to become a bit more 'professional'; to become something that City fans had heard of and wanted to buy. However, I was determined that the fanzine would not lose the innocence and 'amateurism' of the early days, as too many fanzines nowadays are simply replica match-day programmes. One of the outstanding objectives, for me, was that we were to be radical in our content, trying to be a bit different, offering a view of City that would fit in with our perception of being humorous and idiosyncratic, and with a raging hatred of all things 'Manyoo'. I was just the man to offer that. In terms of 'success', the greatest test has been the fact that we have been going three years, having produced twenty-plus issues. We are now into our fourth season of the fanzine (all at different divisions), having overcome a crisis of confidence that almost saw the fanzine cease publication at the end of the 2000/01 season. But after promises of support and encouragement from our 'regulars', we have decided to carry on. That support is probably the most vital factor in the contribution of the fanzine. While I personally do an inordinate amount of work involved with the fanzine, I couldn't survive without the half-dozen regular contributors, or the handful of fellow sellers. It's not that I couldn't carry on, it's just that I wouldn't want to, if no one else was bothered. The fanzine can only succeed if it is 'sparking off', with various contributors sending their own personal views in, or the 'think tank' (the three or four people most closely involved in the production of the 'zine) all sharing views and creating a different outlook than that normally available in other City fanzines. We've been well publicized since we started, with numerous quotes in the *Times* and the *Sunday Times* taken directly from the fanzine. I have been on Radio Five discussing derby matches with the editor of *United We Stand*. I have had Talksport contact me on several occasions for quotes. I've been interviewed on Sky Sports, and even one of the sellers has appeared on Sky Sports talking about the 'lucky straw' we were giving away with one of the issues. He also does the match report for the *Sport First* newspaper. My biggest publicity coup came with the interview I did for the *Times* in their weekly feature on City and their travels in the Division Two, which later made it to the book produced by Mark Hodkinson (*Blue Moon Rising*), from which I was even contacted by Matlow's – the makers of 'Love Hearts' sweets – who provided me with over 1,000 free packets to give away with one of the issues. I also made it onto a Channel Four documentary, talking about my reliance on City and what they mean to me. I had been brought to their attention through the article in the *Times*. I have to admit though, I never feel comfortable doing that part of the job. I always got the impression that the interviews were after an 'angle', looking to portray you in some sad light. I even turned down the Vanessa Feltz show. An offer of an all-expenses paid couple of days in London could not convince me that she wouldn't try

A badge publicizing fans' objections to the proposed ID card scheme. The slogan says it all.

and humiliate me, so I refused. As for the future: in the past I have tried to organize the issues a couple of months in advance, looking for people to fill in the blank spaces, as laid out in advance. I've even produced a number of 'general'-type articles that are not time-limited, enabling me to slot them in when current stuff is a bit sparse. For this season, I am just taking things as I find it. The enthusiasm I had has waned, but so long as other people are prepared to produce stuff, then I will be more than willing to put it all together, but the ego has been mostly satisfied and I have no burning desire to do a book or appear on the radio or television, I will leave that to others more willing. So the fanzine now has a life span of 'the next issue', and so long as it sells enough to pay the suppliers and I still get pleasure from it, we will carry on the frequency of issue. However, the continuity of selling at each and every match may pay the price, as fanzines inevitably diminish in importance due to the internet.

Tom Ritchie

This Charming Fan

I suppose you have to blame the *Manchester Evening News*. In 1984, they published the first letter I wrote to them – and over the next few years, about ninety per cent of letters I wrote to either the *News*, or sister paper the *Pink*, were also published. I discovered I had a talent to write, and they encouraged me to continue, even awarding me £5 prize letters in the *Pink* (the £10 star letter always eluded me!). But then they stopped publishing the letters. My style was changing, and I became frustrated by my letters' non-appearance. I had changed from issues around the team, to issues around the politics of the game. It was now 1987 – two years after Heysal and Bradford, two years before Hillsborough – and Thatcher had made football fans public enemy number one. I had been inspired by a new kind of magazine developing at a small pace – football fanzines. I had remembered buying a few punk fanzines in the late 1970s and early 1980s, and the 'do-it-yourself' idea was now returning, this time with football. *When Saturday Comes* and *Off the Ball* were two fanzines I bought, focusing on national issues, and it was only a matter of time before local club-based 'zines would appear. January 1988 – FA Cup fourth round at Blackpool. Outside I purchased issue number one of City's first fanzine, *Blueprint*. I waited until after number three had come out, before deciding that I liked the style, content and attitude – and spent the next four years writing articles for *Blueprint* and selling it outside stadiums all over the country where City played! It did take over your life: writing to meet deadlines, arriving early to sell, staying behind after to sell, dropping off copies in Piccadilly Records each week. *Blueprint* failed to appear for a few months for a number of reasons – its then editor, Bill Borrows, was busy with other projects on his road to a professional career in journalism, that saw him work for publications such as *90 Minutes*, *Goal*, *Four Four Two*, *Loaded* and the *Daily Telegraph*. I had been producing quite a few articles for *Blueprint*, but with Bill busy elsewhere, nothing was happening. Then I fell out with Bill during the Testimonial dinner for Neil Young in November 1992. Bill had organized the function and had reserved two tables for *Blueprint*. I arrived to find the names of attendees on the table, and was shocked to find I was on the second table alongside people I didn't know, whilst the first table was filled with the main *Blueprint* crew and a few other people who had nothing to do with the 'zine. I had paid £25 to sit on my own. That night, I decided to go it alone and produce my own 'zine. The first name for the 'zine was going back to my punk roots – *God save the Quinn*, in honour of my favourite player, Niall Quinn. I decided against this, as the thought of shouting out the title outside stadiums could be taken the wrong way! The next title fell the same way. Paying homage to David White and the Clash, I think I would have been arrested if I had started shouting 'White Riot' at the top of my voice! Abandoning punk, I gazed upon my collection of Manchester's finest-ever band, the Smiths. Playing a few tunes, 'This Charming Man' came on, and soon I was singing 'This Charming Fan'. At last, I had a title! The first issue really was a DIY job. Other than typing it, I wrote it, pasted all the pages together, and then my mum and me spent a day during the Christmas holidays on her work's photocopier. This was followed by another day collating and stapling it together, before it being on sale for the home cup tie against Reading in January 1993. I took 200 copies and sold them all before the game. Issue one featured two rare editions. Due to a slight mistake whilst photocopying, some pages were printed upside down. Thus, fifty copies were sold with two pages upside down, and – extremely rare – twenty-five copies with four pages upside down! After all 500 were sold, I was about £25 out of pocket, but immensely proud of what I had achieved. Billed as 'The one and only issue', I quickly began writing more articles, and before the end of the season produced the 'Second and last issue'. Again, 500 copies selling out quickly. Over the summer, Bill Borrows wanted to resurrect *Blueprint* and we spoke on the phone, patching things up. I agreed to return, but I wanted to keep my identity, and so *Blueprint* returned – incorporating *This Charming Fan* inside. In the end, *Blueprint* lasted a mere three more issues,

Issue one of This Charming Fan. *Is there room for one more?*

until Bill again became too busy, so in August 1994, *This Charming Fan* – the third and final issue! – came out. I never gave deadlines; a new issue would come out when there was enough to say. This could prove difficult if an issue I had covered was out of date when going to print, but there was enough going on to ensure this was not the case. The good thing with this fanzine is that I was in control, rather than the 'zine being in control of my life! However, by November 1995, it was time to hang up the pen. I had been promoted at work and I now had to do a real job! During my previous role, I was able to produce the 'zine, but not anymore; I was kept busy doing what I was paid to do. Also, I had started to take my eldest daughter to home games and, on one occasion, I arrived early with her and attempted to sell, and it was just too much to expect her to stand there for an hour next to me. December 1995 – the sixth and farewell issue hit the streets and, like all other issues, quickly sold out. The week after I had sold the last copy, I met with friends in a pub and had my first pre-match pint in almost six years – I had forgotten what it was like after all those years stood outside stadiums in all weathers. As I walked past the fanzine-sellers that day – in the pouring rain – I knew I had made the right decision! So, why did I do it? Because I believed in what I was doing 200 per cent and I also enjoyed it. You couldn't do it if you didn't enjoy it. I had something to say and, as no one else would allow me to say it, I said it myself. It was interesting also to see how fanzines had influenced the media, who had now changed their ways to accommodate the new way of thinking. Pre-match and after-match programmes on radio stations and newspapers now featured fan's issues, and if anything happened at a club, the fanzine editor would be the first contacted for an opinion. Fans had become political, and the greatest hour was defeating Thatcher and Moynihan in 1990, over their ludicrous ID card scheme. So, I left the pen behind for good and let a new generation of fanzines take their place in the queue. My time had finished, and for five years I was relatively quiet (well, apart from ringing up Jimmy Wagg on GMR every other week!), until I started to become increasingly despondent about the regulation that stadiums had to be all-seated. In February 2000, I started the campaign SAFE – Standing Areas for Eastlands, the campaign to have safe standing areas in City's new stadium. This has since become a national campaign – Standing Areas for England – with support from all over the country. The new electronic age of the internet means thousands

The sixth and last issue of This Charming Fan.

of fans can be contacted in a very short space of time, at the click of a mouse – no more photocopying and standing outside stadiums in all weathers! This has taken me to a new level, meeting government ministers, being interviewed on national TV and in national newspapers, travelling to Germany on a fact-finding mission, working with other clubs' supporters' groups and meeting the Hillsborough Families Group. It is bloody hard work, and there are times when I question myself as to why I keep getting involved, but as stated before, I believe in what I am doing 200 per cent, and if there is something to say, I just *have* to say it. And I suppose the answer can be found in a quote from a song by the Smiths – 'Is it really so strange? You can kick me, you can punch me, you can break my face – but you won't change the way I feel.'

Phill Gatenby

Issue one of King of the Kippax, *City's longest-running fanzine*.

King Of The Kippax

Why did I ever start this? This is a question regularly asked in the early hours of the morning, as deadline time approaches at alarming speed and the computer's having a tantrum (it's not just a piece of electronic gadgetry you know, it has a personality – and I suspect it's female, rocking along quite amiably until I really, really need some co-operation, when it suddenly goes berserk). Realizing at an early age that I was never going to become a professional footballer, I became a wholehearted football fan (although I was once scouted by United – but my dad chose not to tell me they were watching that day, and I had a particularly stupid, larking around, what-the-hell, let's-chat-up-the-girls-on-the-touchline sort of game – though I like to think I wouldn't have played for them even if they'd asked!). I watched City whenever I wasn't playing, travelling up and down the country on supporters' trains and then entering my 'match reports' in my notebook, so maybe I was always destined to become a fanzine editor. No school homework was ever given the care and attention I lavished on my City diaries. Later I wrote to the newspapers, local and national, or the City programme, whenever I felt there were comments to be made, and was successfully published quite often (once even winning the Dennis Tueart poem competition!). But never often enough, and I was exasperated when some bland letter was printed in preference to mine. In time, I realised that others felt the same. There were more profound comments amongst the fans on the terraces than were ever read in any newspaper or foot-

A more recent issue of King of the Kippax *– the greatest thing since bread came sliced.*

ball publication. Football magazines were aimed at young fans and were generally in the 'what footballers have for breakfast' vein, rather than discussing the politics of the beautiful game. Football fans were not meant to have opinions, they were meant to put up, pay up and shut up. But the times they were a-changing. In the mid-1980s, there was hooliganism, the Heysel disaster, Leeds fans rioting at Birmingham, the Bradford fire, the threat of ID cards, Moynihan (remember him?), Thatcher, away fans banned at Luton, and so on. Reporting throughout the media failed to reflect the experiences of the ordinary football fans who weren't thugs or anarchists, as you might have thought from press reports at the time, but passionate football 'experts' with a valid point of view, which was given little opportunity to express itself. I was reading general football fanzines like *Off The Ball* and *When Saturday Comes*, and in 1987 I joined the Football Supporters' Association, where I was an active member. Encouraged by friends in the FSA, I decided to start a fanzine for my beloved Manchester City, but then met Mike Kelly, who was just starting to put together *Blueprint*, City's first fanzine. He'd beaten me to it. No problem, I thought, I'll just send my contributions to him. However, the first two issues appeared late and out of date, and then on the opening day of the 1988/89 season at Hull, it didn't appear at all, missing the vital deadline. I resolved to do better. My mate Tony offered to arrange inexpensive printing. I borrowed a few quid from the kiddies' piggy bank, and *King Of The Kippax* was born. As you know, it takes its name from that vast terrace, now rebuilt and seated, which was the voice of Maine Road, and Colin Bell, who was the King of the Kippax. Plus it was a fanzine for all Blue-blooded City fans. Sue, my wife, co-editor and illustrator of the 'zine, disliked the name from day one (still does) , and wanted to call it *Kippaxed!* – a fact which she constantly reminds me of, especially when we get accosted on the street with remarks like 'You're not the King of the Kippax, I am!'. Well, I never meant to be that – the fanzine is king, as are all City fans – and when Royle came along, we were able to have the 'Royle Mail' in the royal fanzine, although as he publicly declared he had no time for fanzines, I doubt if he was impressed! K.K.'s here now, of course, and he's agreed to change his name to avoid confusion, but I think that was tongue in cheek! The first ever appearance of *King of the Kippax* was on 24 September 1988. Barnsley away. We won 2-1. I was on my own and I nearly bottled out from selling. But I'd sunk my dosh into it, costs had to be recovered, and, anyway, it was all my own work, and I thought it was a decent read! I sold eighty on the first day at fifty pence a time. Big business! Wow! It was off the ground. For the second issue, I borrowed £400 from the bank for a 'wrap around' professionally-printed job and increased the production run. I wanted to publish regularly, with up-to-date and balanced views, hitting the major issues; reflecting on events; supplying information and, most important of all, providing a platform for fellow fans to express themselves, and they did. The fanzine gradually built up a pool of regular contributors, and sellers too. We also gained a long list of subscribers from all over the world, some of whom we have since met and have become friends with. Over the years, our family and friends have learned to fit in with the fanzine. Births, deaths and marriages have all been scheduled to suit fanzine deadlines at one time or another! The friends we have made through the 'zine are special to us. We've met 'celebs', and helped to make some too – some who have written for us in the past, have been inspired to bigger and better things, which is very gratifying. Being introduced to Norman Wisdom by Rick Wakeman in the Isle of Man was a high point, as was giving Linda Lusardi a smacking kiss when backstage with Eddie Large in Torquay. The most enduring high spot of producing a fanzine, however, is seeing it being read and enjoyed by fellow fans. That makes it all worthwhile. The people we've met through the 'zine, whether high-ranking Maine Road officials, media stars or just fellow supporters, have been a delight to know. On the streets, we're asked the most amazing questions, like 'Have I read this one?', 'Which way is it to the ground?', 'Have you seen my mate, he's wearing a City shirt?', and people outside football have problems understanding what we're about, like the lady in the shop, who when asked if she'd display it on the counter, responded 'Is it a colouring book?' Over the years, we've been involved in the various campaigns – against ID cards, Swales Out, Franny In, Franny Out, Save the 30,000 etc. and we are currently supporting discussions on the merits of safe standing areas. Being asked to appear on the telly when City hits the headlines – usually for all the wrong reasons – is not, as some would think, a particularly enjoyable experience, but when I'm asked, I try to oblige. That's when I wish I had the looks of Richard Gere, rather than Homer Simpson, and I always hope my ex-girlfriends don't see me, to gloat that they made the right decision to pack me in all those years ago. But I do have enough confidence in my own ability to see things through the eyes of the well-informed City supporter, and as such, I accept the challenge, take a big gulp, and go for it. Most people are appreciative, or at least constructively critical (!), but there are obviously the odd few dissenters – we wouldn't be City fans if we all agreed with each other, would we? 'You were well out of order … ' is the usual opening gambit. Interrogation, when possible, invariably reveals they didn't actually hear me on the radio, or see me on TV, just heard about it in a pub somewhere, and basically they think they could have done better. 'OK, pal, when the phone rings, I'll pass them on to you, alright?' No answer. Radio is better as it's usually live, and can't be edited, which can be very frustrating. Conversations with the press can be tricky too, and can lead too much being made of an off-hand remark, whilst the main thrust of the discussion is ignored. Of course, all of this could be edited anyway … ! And then there's litigation, the fanzine editor's nightmare. One ill-considered remark which slips past editorial scrutiny, and there are visions of rendering the family homeless and fatherless overnight. A certain ex-chairman once threatened legal action against a contributor for having implied that there was a booze culture at the club, and we had to apologize profusely, as no such thing could possibly happen at Maine Road, could it? We always think the next issue will be the last. A fellow editor once said that by the time he'd finished getting an issue together, he felt like flushing it down the toilet, he was so fed up with it. There is always that feeling of 'never again', but when it comes back from the printers, all shiny, new and smelling of fresh ink, I can't wait to get out there and sell it on the streets, and as the contributions roll in for the next issue, we're all fired up again, and off we go! The fanzine movement, I suspect, peaked around about 1991, but while some have closed down, new ones are sprouting up all over the place. At City we have four fanzines of excellent quality; each with its own distinct characteristics, and all better than the Stretford Rangers' lot! But then again, I'm somewhat biased. In this time of football plc mania – with official publications on the increase, and access to players and management undreamed of in fanzine circles – whether the 'home-made' quality of the fans' own productions will continue to appeal, is anyone's guess. The average football fan is now being courted by big business like never before. The more the cost of going to a football match increases, the higher the players' wages, the more likely we are to become apathetic, as we realise the clubs with the most money will walk away with the biggest prizes – or will they? This is the beautiful game that we love, and much of its beauty is in its unpredictability, especially at Maine Road.

Dave Wallace

Blueprint

I was fortunate to start following City when the team was winning everything in sight. I've continued to support City through thick and thin – hair! After many highs and lows: a couple of cup finals, a couple of Simod Cup matches, Europe, Halifax, Championship near-misses, Channon near-misses, the pleasure of witnessing the greatest player ever to grace any pitch – Rodney Marsh – and the worst – Mike Walsh – relegation hit home. The first time (1983) it was a shock. The second (1987) hurt. The club had made many mistakes over the years; the greatest mistake of all, though, was taking the fans for granted, to simply use us as turnstile fodder. Relegation gave me plenty of things to think about – Shrewsbury on a Tuesday evening for starters! More than this, it led me to take a closer look at the club I loved, and I didn't like what I saw. A lot of time was spent knowing things had to be said and had to be done – but not knowing what or how to say them. An article in the *Observer* changed all that. The feature was about football fanzines – never heard of them before – and in particular *The City Gent*, a Bradford City fanzine produced by John Dewhirst. This gave me the spark and encouragement to do a similar project at City. An advert was placed in *City Life* and Rob Dunford came on board. Dave Wallace was recruited at a Football Supporters' Association meeting in Manchester, and then Frank Newton, Wilson Pratt and Chris Dawes completed the original line-up. This was the easy part, but getting the nod from the club was proving to be more difficult! To be fair to Swales – and it is hard – it was easy to talk to him, but why shouldn't it have been? Two visits to the club secretary and commercial manager later, a compromise was reached. They stated that

Left: *Issue one of City's very first fanzine*, Blueprint. Right: *The last issue of* Blueprint – *the end of an era.*

the club couldn't support the fanzine, as it might affect programme sales (really!), but they wished me all the best if I decided to continue and go to print. Thanks. But I had decided to go to print long before that point! Worse was to follow with meetings with the secretary of the Supporters' Club. Here was a person who supposedly had the interests of the club's supporters at heart, walking into a meeting with an air of indifference, barely looking at us, hardly listening to us and stating after a couple of minutes of his valuable time that he could never support it, as it might criticise the club! There was a sense, in both its formative years and subsequent evolution, that it bought together City fans of similar socio-political views and opinions and provided a forum for these to be shared, reflected and articulated within the context of football and, in particular, MCFC. And then there was Frank! The City fan who started the inflatable banana craze was a self-confessed Tory – who I am sure only voted this way because of the respective colours of each political party (there is more to it than that, Frank!) – and he was the exception to this typically lefty and unreservedly politically-correct publication. Yet amongst this collection of 'angry and radical young men', there was also humour and laughter along the way. Remember the following? Inflatable bananas; fancy dress parties at Stoke (1988) and Crystal Palace (1990); the plane circling Old Trafford (1991) with the message 'MCFC – The Pride of Manchester' trailing behind; the huge flag that was passed around the Kippax; the 'Blue Moon' 5-1 remix flexi-single that even John Peel played; the Colin

Bell 'Better than Best' t-shirts. These were all funded or promoted through the sales and pages of *Blueprint*. There was the photo we published after the party at Stoke. A group of fans were queuing to go in and one of them was wearing a gorilla outfit. We did the 'face in the crowd' competition and circled the gorilla, offering a cash prize if the gorilla identified himself. We thought it was very funny until this lad kept ringing up day after day insisting it was him and wanted the prize. His consistency in calling paid off, as we eventually gave him the prize – not because we accepted it was him, but just to stop the phone calls! And then there were the Scousers! During 1990, we began a (short-lived) project of making a video diary about the fans throughout the season. It was decided to film visiting fans in the Platt Lane End and the Liverpool game was chosen. This one Scouser spoke at length about how all Scousers were stereotyped and that they were not all unemployed, and told us that all his mates had jobs etc. The next one came along and declared loudly that he objected to the price to get into Maine Road, the price of the pies, programmes and beer. 'We're all on the dole,' he said, pleading, 'how can we afford all this?' in a manner that Harry Enfield would have made a whole series around! And there was the serious side – a donation and floral tributes laid at Anfield after the Hillsborough disaster, a framed photo of the 1934 cup-winning team presented to Alex Williams for his testimonial, and the sponsoring of Fletcher Moss Rangers Under-12s, a junior team from Didsbury. Then there was Frank and Phill Gatenby's brushes with the law and fame on TV! Both were stopped by the police in August 1989, for selling *Blueprint* in the two Kippax tunnels at half-time, photographed and subsequently ejected on the instructions of Mr Swales. And whilst appearing on *Granada Up Front* in February 1990, they managed to handily place a copy of the latest edition over the shoulder of someone being interviewed, much to the annoyance of the glancing disapprovingly Lucy Meacock! By the early 1990s, I took a back seat, as I decided to manage a local band and form a record label. A couple of us even suggested closing down – it was felt such projects shouldn't have longevity and should end at the top – but the majority wanted to continue. So Frank became editor, as a second generation of contributors appeared, such as Bill Borrows (who later became the third editor), Mark Robinson and Andy Webb, amongst others, and not forgetting the unsung work of Chris Dunford as treasurer too. This was one of *Blueprint*'s strengths and made it unique amongst City fanzines in that it wasn't one person who controlled the 'zine,

The party at Stoke – who's a cheeky monkey ?

without whom the whole thing would cease, but contributors came and went and were replaced by newcomers. However, after one brief non-appearance during the 1992/93 season, *Blueprint* reappeared, but lasted another three issues the following season, before finally calling it a day at issue twenty-seven. It was the passing of an era, not necessarily because of the demise – but also in respect of the content and format featured. Was this laddish journalism creeping in? Without a doubt, *Blueprint* had a positive impact on life at Maine Road. At the time of its beginnings, City's fans had a notorious reputation, as 'The Governors' became the first football hooligan gang to be convicted and jailed. The actions of *Blueprint*, whether intentional or not, set the trend for 'softening' the image of fans and bringing humour back onto the terraces, not fear. City themselves, milked the banana craze for every last drop – yet never acknowledged the part played by fans in organizing and promoting it. And on a personal level, there was the ultimate satisfaction of standing on a packed terrace and watching other City fans reading something you have produced. To see fellow Blues laughing – complete strangers – at one's own printed words brings a feeling of reward little else can surpass and reassures you that it didn't matter what the club thought or what other fanzines thought. It was what the fans thought that mattered. And, for six years, *Blueprint* mattered.

Mike Kelly
(Additional information from Rob Dunford)

Chips 'n' Gravy

Chips 'n' Gravy started when I was in fourth year of Ducie Central High School in Moss Side. I got together with another friend who had journalistic aspirations, called Scott Loney, who was about two years older than myself and had taken up an apprenticeship at the *Manchester Evening News* upon leaving school. I had known Scott since the age of about seven or eight, because he lived on Wykeham Street facing the Main Stand, and I lived around the corner on Dorset Avenue (off Thornton Road), and we used to always play football on the street together against the Main Stand wall during the evenings after school. At the weekend, we used to go to the match together – sitting on the Main Stand benches in the earlier years until we were old enough to be allowed in the Kippax on our own at about twelve years old. We used to go away games quite regularly, too – sometimes with his dad, sometimes with mine. His dad (Trevor) and my dad (Arthur) used to drink together in the Social Club for about twenty to thirty years, although we weren't aware of this for the first few years that Scott and I started knocking about. Anyway, as we got older we always wanted to do a magazine about City and eventually *Singing The Blues* was born. It was a real scissors-and-glue production, from which my brother-in-law's brother used to print about 1,000 copies, just charging us for materials. Our first ever issue made its debut at QPR on 2 March 1991 (a game which City lost 1-0 to a Les Ferdinand goal), but my biggest memory (and, somewhat perversely, my highlight) of the game was Neil Pointon getting sent off, because I had written in a 'pen pictures' article on the team that I could see Pointon getting sent off in the not-too-distant future, because of the way he often clips players' ankles when they're running through on goal. Alas, he was sent off for doing exactly that on the very day of its release! In total, we made nine issues of the fanzine over the course of about two years. Scott then got a job with the *Daily Sport* as a sports journalist and still works there now, and with me leaving school and going to college, it all got a bit much and we had to knock the fanzine on the head. Years later, a desire to get involved again led to a conversation in the pub with another mate Pat Corrigan, who I started going out drinking with around the time *Singing The Blues* was coming to an end. He suggested I start up again with him, using his art and design knowledge as a graphic designer with vast Apple Mac experience in his work for *Auto Trader*. We agreed to set the ball rolling after City's relegation at Stoke, with his brother, Les Corrigan, involved in recruiting advertising and selling the magazine. For the first year or so, we had access to all the equipment at the *Auto Trader* HQ in Warrington, but then they started getting a bit funny with us when they realised fully what we were producing, and that they could charge us for use of their facilities, which we simply couldn't afford. Anyway, it's been a bit of a struggle recently, with a distinct lack of contributors and the mag having to pay for its own Apple Mac, which was a real struggle, but we'll continue to produce issues as and when we can, simply because of a love for doing so.

Mike Holden

Bert Trautmann's Helmet

I first started thinking about doing a fanzine when *Blueprint* came out, around about the

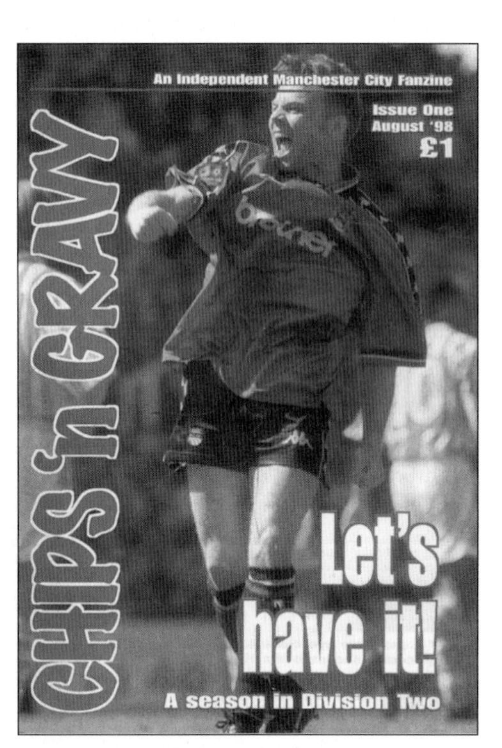

Left: *Issue one of* Chips 'n' Gravy – *perhaps the best-produced fanzine City have had.* Right: A *recent issue of* Chips 'n' Gravy. *Light-hearted relief for the passionate followers of Manchester City.*

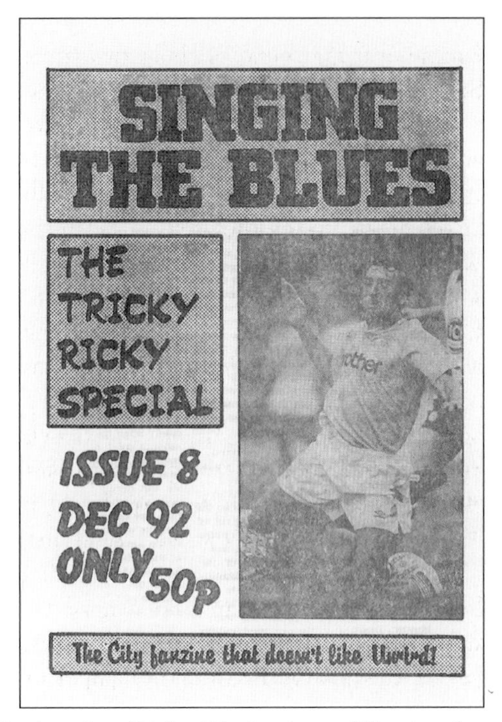

Left: *Issue one of* Singing the Blues. *It fits in your back pocket.* Right: *The last issue of* Singing the Blues – *the 'Tricky Ricky' special.*

end of 1988. I was aware of the fact that there was something from the 1960s called *Out of the Blue*, but fanzines were a relatively new thing, especially when it came to football. I had too much time on my hands, I was out of work, so I thought I would give it a go and see what happened. The first issue came out on 15 April 1989 – City were at Blackburn, but it was also the day of the Hillsborough disaster. It took a while to do, I wrote most of it and asked a couple of mates to contribute. When it came back from the printers, it had been printed on too dark a shade of blue paper, and with black ink, it was almost unreadable. I was amazed people bought it, and it sold out in the first three weeks. When the second edition came out, City were at Bolton, and only 250 copies were ready at the printers. I literally could not get them out of the boot of the car, people were clamouring for them. That's the period I refer to as 'The Golden Era of Fanzines'. After thirty-three issues of *Electric Blue*, a name change was forced upon me. One of the biggest publishers in the country (Northern & Shell) sent me a letter via their solicitors in London. It basically said that they were going to sue me for copyright and infringement, and accused me of damaging the good reputation of their publication, which I found a little bit difficult to believe, but I had access to a red-hot corporate solicitor, and he sorted them out. We made an offer (i.e. a name change) and they accepted it. So, the new name *Bert Trautmann's Helmet* was my choice, and came from the punchline of an old Stan Boardman joke. The name change is not the only problem I have come across in the lifespan of the fanzine. Peter Swales, during his reign, was not very supportive – in fact, it took the club years to realise that we were not attacking them. I have been thrown out of Maine Road, thrown out of Leicester, had fanzines confiscated at Tottenham. I have been moved on by stewards, even council officials, and even to this date, certain fans still think we are taking money out of the club. Producing a fanzine does put you in the limelight though. I have been quoted in such publications as the *Times*. It amuses me because you are held up as some kind of authority, but I regard myself as just being a normal person with a radio face, not TV though. I have turned down Breakfast TV (too early) and *Talking Balls* on countless occasions. The most important thing if you are on TV or radio is to be positive about the club. I personally see the future of *Bert Trautmann's Helmet* as being very bleak. Fanzines have to be put in context with the times. When I started eleven or twelve years ago, there was very little football in the newspapers, it was going through a dark patch. Then *Fever Pitch*, the 'Taylor Report' and the 1990 Italian World Cup started moving things into the twentieth century. For too long, things had dwelt in the nineteenth century. Today you have teletext, radio phone-ins, internet, e-mail, pull-outs in tabloids, magazines by the dozens in shops. It's everywhere. With the advent of desktop publishing and a revolution in technology, I can see somebody going to a match with a palmtop computer, a realtime camera, film the game and relay it back onto the internet via a mobile phone. In a couple of

Left: *Issue one of* Bert Trautmann's Helmet. Electric Blue *comes back into the frame with a different name*. Right: *A recent issue of* Bert Trautmann's Helmet.

years, I will probably look for something else to do. Sales nationwide of fanzines are down. They served a use, but have now got to move with the times or die. I may go out when City leave Maine Road. Although again, come the time, I may find it difficult, you get attached to things. I am just a supporter with a computer, who tries to put in the fanzine, stuff that you would not read any where else: not match reports, but a genuine alternative to anything else available.

Noel Bayley

Although not as prolific as the main fanzines that were produced on a regular basis, City supporters also had access to a number of other City-related publications. Cityzen *was a quarterly magazine, financed and produced by the Supporters' Club. It covered a variety of topics and was edited by former match-day announcer and now local radio personality, Ian Cheesman. Despite the humorous contributions of Fred Eyre, issue two came out a little later than was originally scheduled, and although it was in a new improved format, production ceased after one further issue.* Main Stand View *became the fifth City 'zine, and the first issue hit the streets in August 1991. It was edited by Steve Welch, who had been supporting City from the late 1960s. Even before starting to write the fanzine, he had the minor problem of deciding what to call it . The title he finally settled on was not his original thought, and other options included* Happy to be Blue; Lee, Bell & Summerbee; *and* The Quiet Main Stand. *Steve had been thinking of starting a fanzine for some time, but at first he did not think he had enough material and, although the first issue was amateurish, having been produced on his Brother word processor, it soon sold out and is seen by many as a collector's item. Perhaps the most hard-hitting and controversial fanzine to be produced was* The Fightback. *Dante Friend started it, and the first three issues were very much rough and ready. An A4-stapled production with poor quality pictures. He then began writing articles for* King of the Kippax, *but whilst finding it fun, it was not the same as being your own boss, and after a break of two years, he began producing a more professional issue. He strove to bring outrageous entertainment, but included a few things that got him into trouble and eventually he stopped producing a fanzine altogether. Another fanzine to briefly find itself being sold along side the mainstays was* Blue Murder. *The editor, Francis Fowles, was inspired by* King of the Kippax *and* Electric Blue, *but felt he could produce something fans could enjoy reading and would buy on a regular basis. It also gave him the opportunity to voice his own opinions. Only two issues were ever produced. Francis later returned with* Are you Blue or are you Blind, *which was aimed at the younger end of the fanzine market and wanted it to represent what it was like being a Blue in the eighteen-to-thirty-five age group. Alongside fanzines are the monthly newsletters that are produced by various supporters' clubs, where again, a lot of time and effort is taken by individuals to let people know about the club they choose to support.*

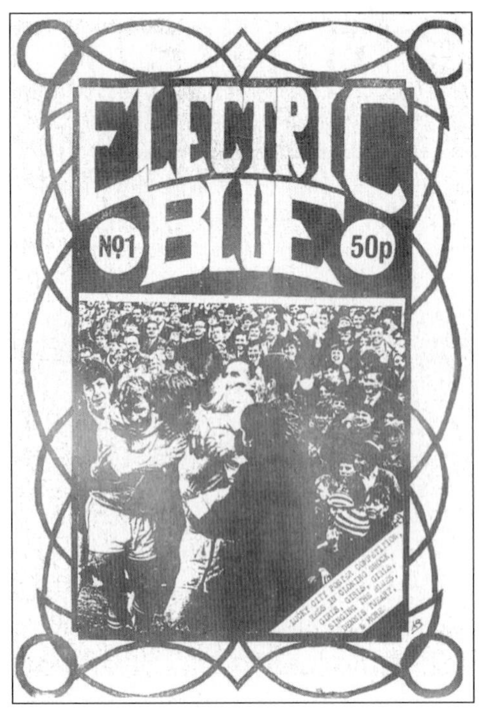

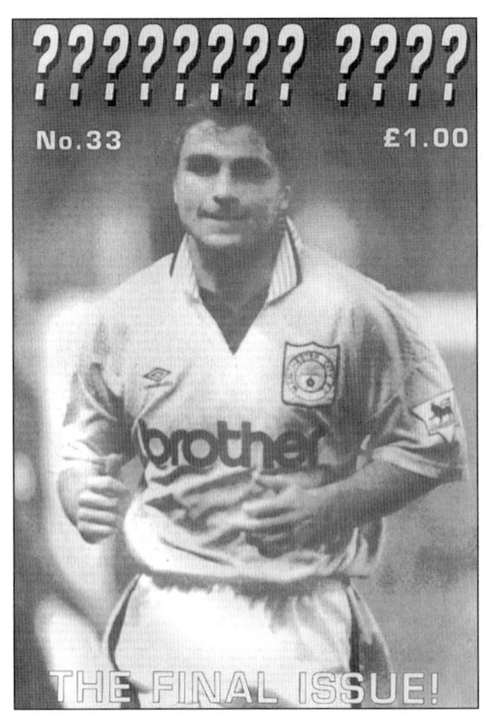

Left: *Issue one of* Electric Blue. *Fifteen bottles of Tipp-ex and two typewriters later, it hits the streets.* Right: *The last issue of* Electric Blue – *the 'zine that dare not speak for itself!*

Left: Blue Murder – *inspired by* King of the Kippax *and* Electric Blue. Right: *Issue one of* Are You Blue Or Are You Blind? – *aimed at the younger end of the fanzine market.*

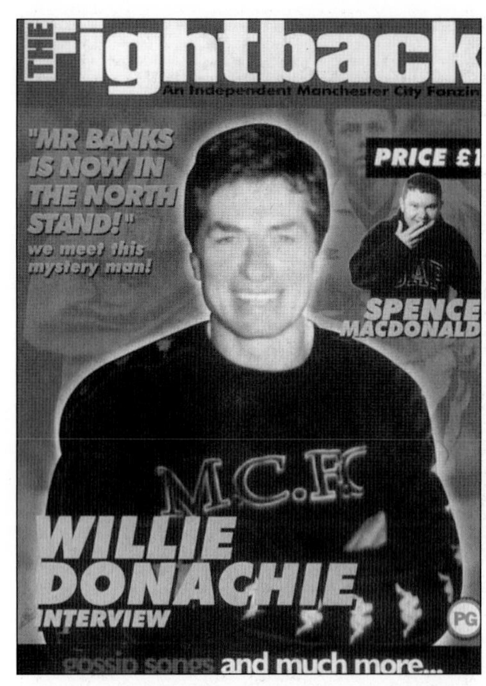

Left: *The old* Fightback *– printing problems beset the first issue*. Right: *New* Fightback *– and then they got it right*.

CITYZEN

THE OFFICIAL MAGAZINE OF THE MANCHESTER CITY F.C. SUPPORTERS' CLUB (1949).

INSIDE INFORMATION

50p

EDITORIAL:
Welcome to what we hope will be the first of many issues of CITYZEN, the new quarterly magazine financed by and produced for the Manchester City Supporters Club.
In this first issue we've got features on a variety of topics which we hope will provoke some response from you Blues fans; your views will be most welcome for the postbag we plan to introduce in our next issue.
As a further dimension to the letters page we plan to get some answers to any questions you might like to ask the officials and players, so get those letters rolling in!
All that and puzzles too, to test those brain cells, and prizes to be won to make it all worth your while.
We hope you enjoy CITYZEN and all being well, we will be back in November. Keep cheering on the Blues!

Ian and Fred.

EYRE SPACE:
Fred's humourous and topical look at City matters.
If you can't wait until our next issue for more from Fred Eyre, we recommend "Kicked into Touch" his brilliant best-selling paperback, republished in August 1989.

BACKCHAT: (Rodney Marsh article)
Backchat this time talks to 70's superstar Rodney Marsh who reflects on his days at Maine Road and his fears for English football.

SOAPBOX:
A chance for a fan to get his or her views on City or a major footballing topic off their chest. If you would like to be our soapbox fan in a future issue, get writing!

FEATURE:
Andy Hinchcliffe and David White talking about their rise through junior football to the First Division with the big boys.

FEATURE:
Mel Machin takes stock after guiding the Blues back to the top.

THANKS:
CITYZEN is edited by Ian Cheeseman and Fred Owen who can be written to at: **Ian & Fred, Manchester City Supporters Club, Maine Road, Manchester.**

We would like to thank the following people for their help, Mel Machin, Andy Hinchcliffe, David White, Rodney Marsh, Fred Eyre, Frank Horrocks, Irene the typist, Jeff Baker and the supporters of City.

The views expressed in this magazine are not necessarily the official opinions or policy of Manchester City F.C. Plc

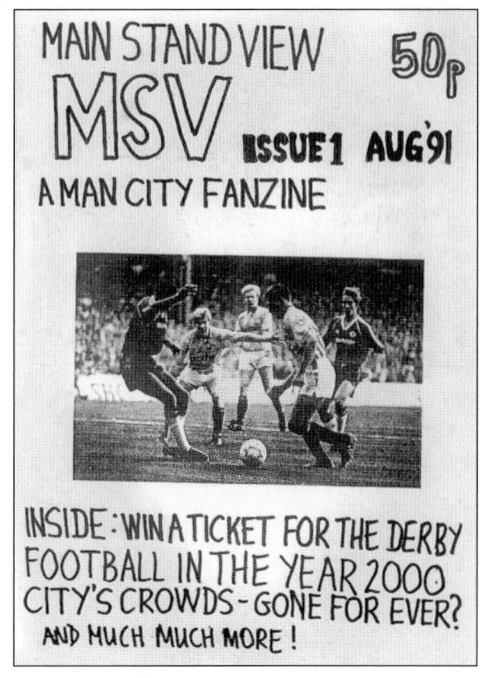

Left: Cityzen *– A quarterly magazine produced by the Manchester City Supporters' Club*. Right: Main Stand View *– the fifth City fanzine*.

Afterword

All of the stories in this book are true accounts, collected in tape-recorded interviews, or through passionate requests in a multitude of City publications.

The stories told by the fans themselves are of real events. The aim has been to bring together a selection of memories, and in so doing, attempt to convey some of the passion and fervour that the fans have for their team.

Manchester City Football Club has a proud history, dating back over more than one hundred years. During that time, the club, spurred on by its loyal and passionate supporters, has reached dizzy heights, and also, it cannot be denied, there have been times of great depression and anxiety. The reminiscences selected and recorded here reflect the variety of these events.

Amidst all the changes, one aspect remains constant, and that is the spirit of the club and its supporters. All fans will enjoy sharing the memories recorded here, and in so doing, will recall many more of their own.

The future: the City of Manchester Stadium, the soon-to-be new home of Manchester City, and the projected venue for the 2002 Commonwealth Games.